DEAR LOVED ONES

An Honest Guide to Helping the Special Needs Family You Love

BY JULIE FALCONE

Note to Readers:

In recounting the events in this book,
chronologies have been compressed or
altered and details have been changed to assist the
narrative. Names and identifying characteristics of
some individuals have been changed.

Edited by Marla Gransworth

Cover Illustration by my talented
daughter, Lucy Falcone

Book Cover Design by pro-ebook cover design

ISBN 978-1-7361335-0-7

First Edition

Dedicated to

Nick, Gabe, Matt, Lucy and Chris

INVISIBLE DISABILITY

/inˈvizəb(ə)l/ /disəˈbilədē/

noun.

"Physical, mental, or neurological condition that limits a person's movements, senses, or activities that is invisible to the onlooker."

~Invisible Disabilities Association

CONTENTS

INTRODUCTION

Raising a child with invisible special needs is HARD. Like, sobbing on the bathroom floor, hard. My husband, Nick and I are raising four children diagnosed with ADHD, autism, sensory processing disorder, anxiety, depression, developmental delay and oppositional defiant disorder, respectively, so it's no surprise that me and my bathroom floor are best friends. It's not just difficult in the obvious ways, like the physical toll it takes on a parent or the extra stress it puts on a couple. The hardest part for me, has always been the mental and emotional side of things. Feeling overwhelmed and living in a constant state of anxiety is exhausting.

Fortunately, we are blessed to have both sets of grandparents, numerous aunts and uncles, cousins, and great friends who rally around us often. Nick and I realize how lucky we are to have such a big support system. Sometimes their help makes things so much easier, and other times, they miss the mark completely. Either way, their hearts are always in the right place.

That being said, even with the most sincere of intentions, our loved ones can never really understand what we are going through or what we need, because they aren't up to their eyeballs in neurological disorders twenty-four-hours a day. Admittedly unfair, I am often annoyed when our friends and family can't read my mind and know just what I need, when I need it. I'll think to myself,

"Can't you see that I obviously need you to grab the baby from my arms so I can calm my uncontrollable toddler who is attempting to bite the dog right now? Ugh!"

"Why do you invite us over, leave your most fragile keepsakes in arm's reach, and then act surprised and upset when someone accidently breaks something? Just put them away before we come. Ugh!"

"Don't tell him to stop flapping his hands when I have told you numerous times that he can't help it. Grrr!"

Intellectually, I know it isn't their fault they don't know exactly what we need at any given moment, but emotionally, I can't help being frustrated at their lack of awareness and basic knowledge of the disorders that plague our family. Between the "help" from my family members and the misguided "advice" from our friends raising neurotypical children, I often feel really alone and misunderstood.

I love our friends and family so much. They are so kind and loving. I realize that these very sweet people don't know what we need because, well, how could they? No one is telling them exactly what would help and what wouldn't. There is no manual for our loved ones to read and learn from.

It became obvious to me that there are SO many family and friends that want to support the special needs family they love. They just need a little insight. I wrote this book because not many people get to see behind the curtain of a mother raising a child with invisible special needs. It isn't talked about because it isn't pretty. Showing the good, bad and ugly side of what my family deals with on a daily basis with ADHD, autism, sensory processing disorder, oppositional defiant disorder, anxiety and depression may be uncomfortable and embarrassing, but I know in my heart, that it will help many families connect on a deeper level. Grandparents, aunts and uncles, cousins, teachers, friends and neighbors can all get a glimpse of our life and use that perspective to be the support their special needs family truly needs.

Trust me, one too many insensitive comments or misguided pieces of advice, whether intentional or not, can mean the end of your relationship with the special needs family you love. It's time to go "all in" and truly immerse yourself in all things invisible special needs.

FROM SQUISHY BUTTS AND BELLY LAUGHS TO DOCTORS AND DIAGNOSES

My husband, Nick, and I celebrated our honeymoon in Aruba. In the hotel, we giggled at the idea of being officially "allowed" to have sex. Both of us were raised Catholic and the thought of not going to hell if we got pregnant was a BIG win for us. We were excited to be married and even more excited to start a family.

Three months after our wedding, we were pregnant! Our first son, Joseph, was born in August and we were over the moon. Twenty-one months later, we welcomed our second son, John, into our family. Twenty-two months after that, we celebrated the birth of our daughter, Ann. A girl! The baby, our fourth and final child, James, was born twenty-two months after her. It was a busy and chaotic seven years.

All I had ever dreamed of was being a mother and I felt like I was exactly where and who I was supposed to be. I was blessed. Don't get me wrong, raising four children under the age of six was a shit show, but it was our shit show and we had it covered.

When I envisioned being a mother, I pictured my children's laughter being heard throughout the house, squishy little butts in the tub, bedtime stories and late-night cuddles. Our reality, however, looked a lot different.

Our youngest, James, was our toughest infant. A definite "momma's boy". The only time he wasn't crying was when I was holding him. He would scream at the top of his lungs, refuse to eat, and make everyone's lives miserable if I weren't available. The minute I would pick him up, the noise would abruptly stop. There were no date nights with my husband or girls' nights out with my friends because babysitters would call within an hour and raise the white flag. I loved that he loved me so much, but there was no reprieve for me.

James' need for me became an issue we had to address because it started to impede his development. Specialists called it an "attachment disorder". It was explained to me that James believed I were an actual part of him, like his arm or leg. He literally thought he couldn't function without me. Part of me was flattered. The other part of me wanted to read a book or go for a run by myself. We started therapy to work on the issue.

In the meantime, we noticed our second son, John, behaving unusually. John was my cuddle bunny. He had always been extra sweet and loving, so Nick and I became worried when we started noticing him becoming quick to anger and throwing tantrums over any little thing. We had assumed it was a phase, but with each year, the phase wasn't ending. His outbursts were exhausting. I would pour cereal and milk in John's bowl for breakfast. He would scream at the top of his lungs, "THAT'S NOT ENOUGH MILK!" I would pour more milk in his bowl and he would throw it across the kitchen at me, yelling, "THAT IS TOO MUCH MILK!" Cereal and milk would GR the counters, floor and my clothes. Imagine that ning multiple times, every day! We started to moods and prayed for this phase to end. for the terrible threes, fours, fives, and no avail. We just kept praying.

this time that I started to unravel. As demands of raising my family were, notional demands that really threw

ty because I wasn't enjoying the had envisioned. I was afraid God rateful. I mean, people I knew divorces and custody battles, es and horrible tragedies and I'm complaining about being tired? To clear my head and try to ground myself, I started running. One mile alone with my thoughts felt good. Three miles alone felt even better. Soon, I was a long-distance runner, clocking over ten miles a day. It wasn't lost on me that I was literally running away from home for hours at a time. Running became my escape when the kids started to become unhinged. It was a survival tactic my body used without me even realizing it.

In fourth grade, my oldest, Joseph, started refusing to get in the car for school in the morning. After weeks of dealing with this, I had it down to a science: If I could drag him towards the driver side of the minivan and push him far enough into the back seat, it would give me *just* enough seconds to jump into the driver's seat, put the car in reverse, push the automatic closed door button, lock all the doors and peel out of our driveway, keeping my speed above 20 miles per hour, there was a chance I could get to school without him jumping out of the moving car or trying to take control of the steering wheel and drive us into a ditch. THIS HAPPENED EVERY MORNING. I knew if I let him stay home just one day, it would make going back even harder for me the next time. I am proud to say I was successful at getting Joseph to school one hundred percent of the time, even if it took six or seven attempts and he wasn't arriving at school until lunchtime. Life was exhausting and I would cry after every painstaking school morning.

He began making comments about there being no point in living. Nick and I were scared to leave him alone for fear he might hurt himself. Before long, his threats of suicide escalated and after many desperate phone calls, we finally got him in front of a psychiatrist and had him evaluated. The doctor put him on an antidepressant for his depression and a stimulant for his newly diagnosed ADHD. It really helped and he turned the corner, thank God!

A year later, John followed the exact same path of school refusal, showing signs of depression, anxiety, and intense rage. As John's aggression grew worse, so did his depression. My cuddle bunny, who would suffocate me in hugs and kisses and constantly tell me he loved me, was gone. His personality completely changed. He only spoke to us or looked us in the eyes if he had to. There were no more hugs or kisses. We "lost" him to depression for over two years. The change was so dramatic and happened so quickly that there was no preparing for it. There is a piece of my heart that is broken from that time that will never mend.

After many evaluations, John finally got diagnosed with ADHD, depression, anxiety, sensory processing disorder and oppositional defiant disorder. With the proper medication and tons of family therapy, he has learned skills to manage in a world where he often feels uncomfortable. Some things are still hard for him. He has trouble showing affection and being vulnerable. Sadly, John hasn't told me he loves me in over four years. To feed my heart, I take his playful teasing as his way of displaying his love for me. I'll take it. I'll take anything that he will give me because I desperately need to connect with him. Sometimes, without meaning to, he will let his guard down and I'll catch a glimpse of his good heart. God does that just for me.

With two kids diagnosed with ADHD, I made it my job to know everything about the disorder. I read every book, attended conferences as far as twelve hundred miles away, and joined every related organization to gain as much knowledge as possible. Nick and I participated in seminars, classes and retreats to learn how to raise our children in an environment that promoted growth and encouragement.

During all of this, my daughter Ann continued to be my breath of fresh air. She is easy going and sweet and brings me pure joy. Ann recognizes the many moods of her brothers and responds accordingly. She is a neurotypical child surrounded by siblings who are anything but. However, I have diagnosed her with being one bad-ass BOSS!

When my older boys started to hit their stride, I could concentrate on my "wild-child", James. His attachment to me was still significant and we were inseparable. I think I started to need him as much as he needed me. But, my "mommy radar" started blowing up after a legit tantrum over snow pants. I knew I had to get some answers. After many different doctors, tests, and evaluations, James was diagnosed with autism, ADHD, anxiety, sensory processing disorder, and developmental delay. I could handle ADHD. Hell, I was an expert in ADHD. I had a grip on anxiety and depression too. But, autism? That was when I threw in the towel.

When I prayed to God to make me a mother, I didn't mean this. I didn't mean a mother who had to work SO damn hard just to keep her family above water. I was overwhelmed. I told God I wasn't strong enough to help this beautiful child. I wanted to give up. Interesting fact: time didn't stand still during my pity party. The world kept turning. My kids still needed lunch and clean clothes still needed to be transferred from the washer to the dryer. So, life went on, which meant, so did I.

I got to work learning about autism. I read how important early intervention is and advocated for James to get occupational therapy, physical therapy, and applied behavioral analysis as soon as possible. I learned how to make visual schedules and daily routines, so he could feel more in control. I worked with him on getting dressed and respecting personal space. I enrolled him in equine therapy. I hit my stride and felt powerful again. We were going to be Ok.

Throughout all of this, my husband was busting his ass at work to provide for us financially. It was not easy for him to go from a stressful work environment immediately into a stressful home scenario. Before even walking through the doorway, his patience was thin and his frustration tolerance low. Yelling and exasperation followed right behind him. This wasn't how he envisioned his family life either. We worked with the family therapist on successfully co-parenting our special needs kids. We never gave up on each other, even when we wanted to. And believe me, there were many times we *really* wanted to. Relationships are never easy, but with our strong faith and commitment to each other, we are still trucking. I'm pretty damn proud of us.

My family has definitely come a long way from where we started. At publication, I have a fifteen, thirteen, eleven, and nine-year-old. My life is still a mess. The laundry is piling up, and my hair hasn't been washed in God knows how long. I still have my baby weight and that "baby" is nine years old. Life is still chaotic and I assume it always will be. Life as a "mom of children with invisible disabilities" will always have its ups and downs. A lot of downs, really. The "ups" will always be the actual children who, no matter how annoying, are amazeballs. Joseph makes me laugh constantly. John is tough on the outside but a teddy bear on the inside. Ann is small, but mighty and will kick her brothers' butts when she has to. James is so adorable that I can never stay angry at him no matter how many times he breaks my Mac Computer (the running total of electronics broken: 4 Macs, 1 Ipad, 2 phones).

This is all to say, life changes quickly. One minute we were pinching our son's little hiney and the next we were learning words like, "sensory processing disorder" and "oppositional defiant disorder." Even though our child's behavior was the same after we received his diagnosis, our family dynamic changed completely. With knowledge comes power, with power comes responsibility, and with responsibility comes stress and fear of screwing it all up.

Dear Loved Ones,

We didn't envision our child having special needs. This is not what we were expecting. We pictured blowing raspberries on our baby's belly and the hardest part of parenting being the sleep deprivation. This is not what we had in mind and it was not an easy pill to swallow. In fact, it rocked our world. But, we love our child and will move mountains to help him.

Our lives are harder than you could imagine. We are most likely drowning.

Often, we feel like crappy mothers who are screwing up our kids. We want to quit this job more often than not. We were not taught how to raise a special needs child and feel utterly unqualified for this job. Please know that behind our smile, there are tears.

Talk to us. Peel back our layers and see us struggling. This life is hard—too hard sometimes. Just by you knowing this, helps. Say a prayer for us when you see us. We need it, for sure.

Tell us you are reading this book. It will help us realize how much you love us. We will see you in a different light when we find out you are trying to understand our lives. It is a sweet gesture that will surely not go unnoticed.

We will appreciate it more than you could even know.

Thank you.

WE WISH YOU KNEW

I recently attended a lecture with other "special moms" to learn different tactics on making transition from one activity to another easier for our anxiety-ridden children. Honestly, I didn't hear the speaker's words after the first five minutes of his speech. (So sorry, sir.)

When the psychiatrist first stood at the podium, he asked the audience to indulge him in an exercise.

"Raise your hand if you are a single parent."

A bunch of hands went up.

"Raise your hand if you are co-parenting in a divorced family."

Many hands went up.

"Raise your hand if your child is nonverbal."

Hands up.

"Raise your hand if your child is aggressive and physically hurts you."

Hands up.

"Raise your hand if you have more than one child with

special needs."

Hands up.

"Raise your hand if you and your husband are living under the same roof but not thriving."

Hands up.

"Raise your hand if your special needs child is adopted."

Hands up.

I looked around at those hands—all those women—and thought of the different challenges we were all facing. Here are some of the things these special moms wish their loved ones knew about their everyday lives:

The single Mom

This woman works all day, pays all the bills, does all the wash, makes all the meals, sets up all the therapy appointments, goes to said therapies, and does morning routine and bedtime routine. And then, she gets up and does it all over again the next day! She is exhausted, both emotionally and physically, and feels lonely most days.

She wants to share these responsibilities with someone. It is too much for any one person. She wants to slump on the couch next to a partner who validates her and tells her how strong she is.

The "Working Outside the Home" Mom

This woman works her ass off to take care of the kids and works outside the home. She is in charge of everything. She gets herself showered and dressed and the kids up, fed, and ready for school. She gets them to the bus stop with lunches in hand and puts in a full day at work, hardly breaking for lunch. She comes home, makes dinner, feeds the family, cleans up, gets the kids in the shower, and puts them to bed. This woman emails the teacher about issues at school, hires the sitter for the date night she is planning for her and her husband.

She feels like she is not doing well at home or at work. She feels like she is failing her family and her boss. Every. Single. Day.

The Mom with the Nonverbal Child

She would give anything to hear her baby say, "I love you." She would love to be able to help her child communicate with not only her but other people. She wants her child to have friends, but that doesn't seem likely. She prays and begs God that the speech, occupational and physical therapies will help her child make words. It is all such hard work. She cries all the time and feels so alone.

The fact that her child can't verbally validate all her hard work with a whispered, "Mommy, you are the best," is destroying her.

The Mom with a Verbally Abusive Child

This mom gets berated daily by her impulsive child. He tells her that she is stupid, dumb, and fat. He screams curse words at her and tells her what a horrible mother she is. She tries to get away from him, but he follows her around the house, calling her an idiot. She tries to ignore him and reminds herself that it is his ADHD talking and not her beautiful boy. But every word he speaks is etched in her heart and pounds away at her fragile, uncertain mind.

She walks around pretending not to hear him scream how much he hates her and wishes she were dead. Her eyes look empty and tired. She is spent and broken inside.

The Mom with More than One Child with Special Needs

She doesn't have a chance to celebrate the victory of one of her children's occupational therapy milestones, because she is stopping the other one from getting into the medicine cabinet. She can't give affection or attention to one child in need without guilt about not taking care of the other. She is exhausted and wonders why she was given more than one child who has special needs. Once she has one of her children's meds figured out, the other goes off the rails and she is back in crisis mode. She can't hide from invisible special needs even for a minute. She doesn't get to breathe without worrying about the safety of one of her children. There isn't a moment when she can just sit on the couch and peruse a magazine, because the second she looks away is the second someone falls or gets hurt.

She feels sad and lonely on the inside. She questions how this became her life.

The Mom with One Special Needs Child

This mom is EVERYTHING to her child. Not just caregiver but friend, therapist, and teacher. This woman doesn't get to say, "Go play with your brother," to get a break. The only person for her child to play with is Mom. So, she builds another fort, colors another page, and watches the same movie forty times in a row. Her life is her child, and it will be the two of them forever. There is no other child to tell her she is doing a great job. There is no way to know what it would be like to raise a neurotypical kid. She lives only in this autism, anxiety, ADHD, sensory processing world day in and day out. She is lonely, even though she is sitting next to her seven-year-old.

So, it doesn't matter what situation we are in. We are all tough, strong women who are taking what we have been given and making f*cking lemonade. The grass is not greener. It is not harder or easier for one family than another. Raising a child with invisible special needs takes everything we once were and turns us into a completely different person. A "special mom" is fierce, and, as hard as life is, we couldn't love our children any more than we already do. We will do anything and everything for them.

Dear Loved Ones,

It wouldn't be better if we stayed with our husband or if we got a divorce. It wouldn't matter if we had money or didn't. If my child's needs were less or more extreme than another's, that wouldn't change things. We are raising children with special needs and there is not one, right way to do it.

Please understand that, no matter what situation we are in, we are doing our best. It is not always fun, and it is definitely not easy, but we are trying and working with what we have.

Be gentle with us. We are so tired and so fragile. We are a battered parent. We cry in our closets, in the shower, and in the car. We wonder if we can continue. We question our mothering skills. We question everything.

Text us, call us, drop us a note telling us that we are a good person. Remind us that we are strong, and we've got this. Just keep reminding us how great we are for our child. Tell us every time you see us that we are your hero. Tell us we are the best mom you know.

Little by little, we may start to believe you.
Thank you.

"ADHD IS JUST A FOCUS THING... NO BIG DEAL."

John, my second son, was eight years old when we noticed his symptoms. He wouldn't sustain eye contact, smile, or make any type of connection, physical or emotional, with my husband and I. He wore hoodies to hide his eyes from the world and only spoke when it was required. He would neither give nor receive affection of any kind. He was so obviously in a bad way, and it broke me.

I took him to every doctor and therapist I could find. I was trying to discover what was "wrong" with him. His anger was so strong and scary. My husband and I call that time period "The Lost Years". We truly lost him. I wanted so badly to make him better and bring him back to us, but I was not qualified to know what was going on or how to help him.

One afternoon, we went to meet a new therapist. The drive there was awful. John was throwing car seats at me, screaming over and over, "You're an idiot. You're an idiot. You're an idiot." Tears were streaming down my face as I videotaped him with my phone.

I showed the video to the therapist. He immediately told me that John needed to see a neurologist. He explained that John wouldn't be able to succeed in therapy at this point, because he was not in the right mindset to even participate in it. After waiting weeks to get in to see the neurologist, who didn't take insurance (no surprise there), we finally sat down in his office and I showed him the video.

The specialist took one look at the video and said, "He has ADHD." I immediately responded, "Um, no, he has no trouble focusing and no issues at school. Look at the video again, please."

That's the day I learned everything I thought I knew about ADHD was so wrong! ADHD IS ABOUT SO MUCH MORE THAN FOCUS! I left his office and did what any sane person does when a diagnosis is made: Google it, of course!

I found a YouTube video of Russell Barkley, one of the nation's leading authorities on ADHD, explaining my son's diagnosis in terms I could understand. I stayed up all night watching this man talk about what happens when ADHD is uncontrolled.

Holy Shit! I cried, no wailed, during the entire three-hour video. Drug addiction, teen pregnancy, car accidents… all things kids with ADHD have a much higher chance of happening to them than their peers who do not suffer with ADHD. I had never heard of the impulsivity side of ADHD. That YouTube video turned my world upside down.

This was not just a focusing issue. This was going to be a lifetime of managing and controlling symptoms. A lifetime of my son trying to stay regulated, so he didn't do something impulsive, making a mistake that could ruin his life. All of a sudden, the thought of my kid with a driver's license scared the shit out of me. Drugs for some kids can be experimental or recreational. For mine, the chances of it leading to a life of addiction were higher than those for your average "pothead".

To those people who say, "Oh, ADHD? Yeah, everybody has a little of that in them," or "Oh, I'm sure my son has that, too," I have something to tell you: No. No, your son doesn't have it if he gets a little rowdy or hyper after eating too much cherry fun dip. Hey, dipshits, this is life-threatening, and it is f*cking scary. Russell Barkley tells us, "Having unmanaged ADHD makes you three times more likely to be dead by age forty-five." An article published in JAMA Pediatrics reports that teens with ADHD are four times more likely to get in automobile accidents. Another alarming statistic from an article published in the Journal of the American Academy of Child & Adolescent Psychiatry states, "Twenty-five percent of adults treated for alcohol and substance abuse also have ADHD." No, this is definitely NOT just about focus.

This diagnosis is life-changing for the whole family. Russell Barkley warns that untreated ADHD leads to "a tenfold increase in teenage pregnancy" as well as more frequent and serious car accidents, financial issues, with more credit card abuse and debt. Sustaining relationships is hard for people with untreated ADHD, leading to higher divorce rates. Another scary statistic from Dr. Barkley is that thirty-five percent of teens with unmanaged ADHD drop out of school. These are not pretty statistics. When I learned these facts, I realized how serious this disorder is.

It isn't as simple as taking a pill and moving on, either. This is a lifetime of therapy and medical management. It is so much more than I ever could have imagined and a trillion times harder than I was ready for. This shit is real, and it is scary.

This is what happens with most invisible special needs. We think they are no big deal until someone we love is diagnosed. Then we learn how devastating these disorders can be to not only the afflicted but also to their family. Anxiety, oppositional defiant disorder, autism, sensory processing disorder, ADHD, and other invisible special needs are so much more complex than you could imagine.

Dear Loved Ones,

Don't underestimate this diagnosis.

It is false to think ADHD, or any of the other invisible special needs are "not that big a deal."

Don't tell us that our doctors got it wrong. We know our children better than anyone, and we wouldn't accept a diagnosis we didn't believe in. Questioning our judgement about what doctors we go to or how we choose to treat our child's diagnosis is insulting.

Educate yourself on whatever diagnosis we are attending to. By learning about it, you will be less likely to say something insensitive. Also, we will appreciate that you are trying to understand our kid and our struggles. Learning about our kid's diagnosis would be a beautiful way for us to feel your support.

Understand the gravity of what we are dealing with each day. Come to us and say, "OMG, I was reading an article about childhood anxiety, and I didn't realize how paralyzing it can be. That must be so hard for you AND him. If he's Ok with it, we would love to have him sleepover this Friday night." To say that would make us feel so loved and supported is an understatement.

Usually, we are dying inside, and every ounce of kindness from you makes us feel hopeful that maybe we are being understood and seen.

Thank you.

WHAT DID I DO WRONG?

I am pretty confident that every mom raising a child with special needs, visible and invisible, has asked themselves the question: "What did I do wrong?" We have racked our brains trying to figure out what it is that we did wrong during our pregnancy that gave our angel this disorder or disease. We all think it. I know for a fact that my gene pool didn't give my children a fighting chance at being mentally stable. Sorry kids, my bad. (Better yet, let's blame Grammy and Poppy!)

By not catching John's ADHD symptoms earlier, did I miss an opportunity at getting him interventions sooner that would have changed his outcome? There were years when my eldest son struggled in school, and I just assumed he wasn't trying hard enough. It never crossed my mind to have him evaluated for ADHD. I was not fighting for 504 plans or IEPs. Instead, I was fighting with my child to pay attention and do better! By not getting the resources he needed sooner, did I waste years of his life that he could have excelled in school, felt proud of himself, and had better self-esteem?

Did I scar my son when I screamed at the top of my lungs, "Stop making my life so hard!" because I couldn't handle one more disrespectful outburst that oppositional defiant disorder is known for? Will my daughter be in therapy for the rest of her life, lamenting about her mother never giving her enough attention because Mommy was always working with her brothers?

There is about a 90% chance my kids will blame me for most things in their lives. Truth is, I probably have ruined parts of my children at some point in their lives, and they haven't even hit puberty yet! But if I ruined them, it was out of love. I hope they see it this way: "I loved you enough to ruin you. So, children, if I were you, I'd get a good job with great insurance benefits to help pay those therapy bills!"

Dear Loved Ones,

Please don't imply that we were the cause of our child's issues. Don't ask us if we breastfed him when he was born. Don't ask us if we ate lunchmeat or soft cheeses during our pregnancy. Don't insinuate that we are parenting them wrong or that these issues are our fault. (When my mother was pregnant with me, she drank alcohol and smoked cigarettes and I came out Ok-ish). Don't ask if we got our child vaccinated, and then shake your head at us with disappointment and judgement when we answer.

We do not need anyone making us feel worse than we already do. Just don't do it, man. If you are thinking any such thoughts, stuff them down your mouth, smile, and move right along.

We don't need to hear those words.

Thank you.

FLEXIBLE SHMEXIBLE

It can be hard for kids with invisible disabilities to be flexible. Inflexibility can be pretty tough for my family of six. "So, I know we said we were going bowling, BUT the bowling alley had a flood, so we are going to the movies instead." Cue hysteria. They don't care that I just spent $100 on movie tickets, or that I bought gallons of popcorn (that will clog several arteries) for another $100.

They care that I told them we were going bowling. "You are the worst mother ever! You ruin everything! I hate everything that you are! By the way, you're fat AND stupid!" Even as we take our seats in the theater, they are acting like jerks and can't get over the change in plans. So, I am $200 poorer, and everyone is still miserable. Awesome.

This rigidity can be embarrassing when we are out in public. No one else's kid is flipping shit in the ice cream parlor because they are out of chocolate s'more ice cream. Other people's children are sitting on the bench, happily licking their cones. Not my kid. I take my hysterical son aside and quietly try to talk him down. But there is no rationalizing his devastation over this seemingly, small problem. I'm talking no joke, my-dog-died devastation.

During the tantrum, I feel bad that my little boy is flipping out. I mean, it's not his fault that he is so rigid. I also feel bad for me because no other mother is on her knees, begging for eye contact so she can get him to calm down.

So, I take him to find an ice cream parlor that does have chocolate s'more ice cream on tap. It makes me sad we had to find a different place. He is no longer with his peers enjoying ice cream and socializing. It is just him and me. In fact, it makes me so sad that when we do score chocolate s'more ice cream, I order a double with extra whipped cream for myself and eat my emotions in the front seat of the car.

While I am going over the scene in my head, critiquing what I did and what I should have done differently, my cutie happily eats his cone as if nothing at all has just gone down. He's over it and has moved on. He hasn't thought about those other kids once. He got his s'more ice cream. The end.

Unfortunately, I have not moved on.

I can't let "ice cream-gate" go, because there are lost social opportunities like this happening all too often. You know the moments: being at the ice cream parlor with friends, going to Johnny's party, or playing capture the flag at the park with a group of kids. He is not a part of any of that. It hurts my heart to accept that. But he doesn't know, or care, that he has missed out on these moments. He is living his own life, and everyone else is irrelevant. Flexibility, or the lack thereof, is inconsequential to my son, but it is super difficult for his family to deal with.

I ask myself often, "If he is happy, why do I care what his social status is?" He's not crying in the corner that he isn't invited to every party; he's fine with it. I need to learn to be fine with it, too. Easier said than done. This is my baby we are talking about!

Dear Loved Ones,

Sorry we can't randomly stop by to say hi, even though we are passing right by your house. Don't make us feel bad about it. Trust me: you wouldn't want us there anyway, because you and I wouldn't be able to talk over the screaming. "Why is he screaming, you ask?" Because he is supposed to be home right now watching Ben 10, Episode 4 (the same one he watches every afternoon at this time).

Don't get mad at us when we respectfully decline your dinner invitation because you are having Italian. For us, Wednesday is Chinese night. Just know that we wish we could be there. It would have been nice. So, instead of taking things personally, just tell us that you will be happy to see us whenever we can make it.

Friends, don't get angry that we haven't been to anything social lately. We are living the same day over and over because it works for our kids. Don't ask us to apologize for that. Just give us a pass. Don't make us feel bad about it. Imagine being stuck in the Groundhog Day movie where each day is the same. It is what the kids need, but that doesn't mean we, the parents, like it.

It can be very depressing to live this way. We are sad and lonely when we miss opportunities to visit with friends or family. It hurts more than you could know. Ask us what day and time would work for you to come visit us. That way, our kids won't lose control because they are in their "safe" environment, and we can still be together!

Tell you what, you bring the Chinese this Wednesday night!
Thank you.

HELLO, PRINCIPAL

Another call comes in. I know the number by heart. The dreaded school phone number. I cringe every time that number shows up on my caller ID! I never know who it will be about, but my heart instantly sinks. Is it my eldest, Joseph, who decided to write, "I hate f*cking math" on his algebra test, or is it John, who threw a highlighter through the school bus window? Did James draw on his reading partner? It's anybody's guess. Truth be told, as I am writing this, I just got interrupted by a phone call from the school (no joke). One of my children decided to make his own art: his test paper is filled with a million different kinds, sizes, and colors of penises. Yep. That's about right.

My husband has zero tolerance for these calls. He is furious before the principal is even finished talking. He has a punishment already in his mind that will teach our son a lesson. My poor husband is infuriated with steam coming out of his ears! He is hardwired to have this reaction. It is in his genes, really. I get it. It's not my style, but I get his first reaction to this call.

My husband will say things like, "When I was his age, I was scared of my dad." I understand this because I had a respectful fear of my dad, too (and his belt). We come from a time when smacking and hitting your kid wasn't a big deal. My dad would give us the belt when we deserved it, and we turned out Ok. That's just not the way it works today. (Not sure if that is a good thing or not).

I am often described as being "too positive and soft" because I will immediately give my son our support, no matter what. That doesn't mean I condone his actions. It just means I don't yell at the top of my lungs about the situation. Instead, I will hear the principal out. I will spend the rest of the afternoon racking my brain, trying to figure out what my beloved child must have been thinking when he drew this "art". How did his lack of executive functioning mess with him today? Was it his impulsiveness? Was it that he was feeling less than the other students, for some reason, and acted out? Or was he just being a stupid teenager? I am like a loving detective trying to figure out the "why" and "how" of the situation. Truth be told, we will never know why he does half the things he does because he, himself, doesn't know.

I can be calm and see the big picture. In fact, after this incident, I told my husband, "He has come so far. Last year, he would have drawn those penises on another kid's face!" He didn't find that funny. I try to remind him how far our son has actually come. Last year was a complete shit show, so this feels like small potatoes to me. Last year, he wouldn't even walk into the school building! Now, he not only goes in but is participating in art!

Of course, we still punish them by making the

penis culprit and the captain of Highlighter-Gate write apology letters to the principal, teachers, and the bus driver. We take their phones away and explain what we expect from them. We sit them down and say the same thing we always beg, I mean, say, "Just keep your head down, do your work, and come home. That's it." I try to tell the kids that, as much as I like their teachers and principals, I don't want to be on their speed dial!

I have learned a lot from the numerous phone calls I have received in the past ten years. I used to listen to the teacher and believe that she knew best. I used to automatically support her decisions about consequences and discipline. I did that until one particular phone call came in and I betrayed my son. He had pushed a boy down the hill at recess. The boy had special needs. When I heard this, I wanted to curl up and die. What kind of monster was he? What was I supposed to do with this kid? The principal told me she believed my son lacked empathy and should see a therapist. She took away my son's recess for two weeks. She sounded disgusted. I felt ashamed. I thanked her profusely and agreed with everything she said. I told her we would take care of this at home.

Later that afternoon, my son came home, and I started yelling at him before he was even in the house. He was mortified at what the principal said about him. He told me what happened. First, he didn't know this boy had special needs because they were invisible. (How ironic.) While they were playing football, the boy kept trying to push my son down the hill. My son said he told the boy to stop a bunch of times, that he just wanted to play the game. Then after a while, when it wouldn't stop, my son pushed him back.

After listening to his side of the story, I felt ashamed. I had betrayed him. I had told the principal I agreed with her judgements, without even talking to my son first. I should have told the principal that I would talk to my son and get back to her. Then I could have defended my son. I am supposed to be his biggest supporter, and I had let him down.

Cue self-hatred and self-disgust. For weeks after that incident, I cried because I was so disappointed in myself. I let my beautiful baby down. Since then, I always listen to both sides of the story and the teachers and I come up with a plan of action that we can agree on.

I am done throwing my kids under the bus. I am their advocate first and foremost.

Dear Loved Ones,

We want to confide in you about what our kid did at school that almost got him suspended. We feel scared, alone, tired, and have NO clue what to do about it. Be prepared: the story will be bad. You will immediately do two things after you hear it: 1) hug YOUR child so tight, grateful that he didn't do such a thing, and 2) want to tell us, in a delicate tone of voice, to call the closest military or boarding school we can find.

OK, get your shit together! Please, put your eyes back in your head and pick your jaw up off the floor. We are so embarrassed and fear you are thinking we are failing as mothers. When you hear the awful story, just listen with a very neutral face. Then tell us how you believe the principal over-reacted and, unless our son threw a CHILD holding that highlighter out the bus window, it doesn't sound like a huge deal. Remind us that you know our child and know he has a good heart.

Try to calm us down. Reassure us that every person makes mistakes. Tell us that we are actually lucky because our kids are making small mistakes now, as opposed to big mistakes later in life. Remind us to be compassionate and forgiving to our child. Remind us to be compassionate and forgiving to ourselves as well.

Hug us and tell us that our kids are awesome, and we are good parents. Tell us that there are worse things in the world than a suspension from middle school (whether you believe it or not).
Thank you.

STOP STARING AT ME, BITCHES!

Nothing makes me hate myself more, as a mom of a special needs kid, than when I see, no FEEL, the beady, judgmental eyes of other mothers, grandmothers, teachers, or neighbors while my kid is in the middle of a tantrum. Yes, lady in the bleachers, I am talking to you. Yes, I KNOW I shouldn't be carrying my child onto the baseball field as he hits, kicks, and pulls my hair out. I know it looks like I am torturing him. I also know that he <u>hates</u> transition. If I can get him into the dugout, there is a 25% chance he will remember how much fun he had batting in the last game. So, lady, STOP STARING AT ME!

You have no idea how many hours of therapy and doctors' appointments we have been through to get us to this point. You have no idea that last baseball season, he wouldn't get out of the car, and we watched his team play from the parking lot. You don't know that getting him into the dugout is a HUGE accomplishment. STOP STARING

AT ME!

It looks like I am giving in to him when I buy him a slushy JUST to get him to put his baseball pants on. What is that you say, lady? That is bribery? Well, I call it behavioral reinforcement. Kiss my butt.

My youngest son, James, is diagnosed with sensory processing disorder. A symptom of this is that he doesn't feel cold the way others do. Parents give me disgusted looks and tsk-tsk-tsk when they see my kid show up to school in shorts and a t-shirt on snowy, frigid days. "What kind of mother lets her child out like that? I would MAKE my kid wear a coat."

Shut up, lady. Shut up. Shut up. Shut up!

All three of my boys suffer with ADHD. They have trouble expressing their anger appropriately. Unfortunately, their default is usually violence. When they were between two and five years old, it was annoying when they would hit and kick me, but I managed. Between nine and twelve years old, they have grown bigger and stronger and it can be downright dangerous! So, imagine what the beady-eyed women are thinking when they see me trying to restrain my preteen at a football game to keep him, and those around him, safe. I am in full crisis mode, sweating my ass off as I try to hold this one-hundred-pound person down. I am quietly crying and whispering, "I love you," softly in his ear.

I can hear it now: "He just needs a good ass whooping." "I would NEVER allow my kid to disrespect ME like that." Seriously, shut up and STOP STARING AT ME!

Judgements by other mothers, grandmothers, cousins, friends, and strangers are everywhere. They are at the ball field, the grocery store, and school. Pick any place, and I will likely be getting judged for my child's behavior. These awful stares follow me around and seep into my mind, even though I swear up and down that I don't care what anybody thinks. Dumb people with their dumb judgments: I hate your stares that scream, "you suck" drilling into my back.

John decided, in the middle of the football season, that he no longer wanted to play. No matter what we said to him, he was sticking to this decision. At that time, I hadn't yet learned the skills to handle him in a situation like this. And even if I had, I am not sure I would have dealt with it correctly, anyway. It is so easy to forget what I am supposed to do! What did the therapist say I should do again?

So, cut to: me dragging my third grader, in full football pads, to the middle of the football field, in front of his teammates and coaches. I thought he would stop fighting me if he knew people were watching. I was wrong. Instead, the second I let him go, he ran off the field like a wild animal escaping the zoo. As I stood there, quietly crying (my flip-flop-clad feet had been stepped on by his cleats the entire time), I saw and felt the stares and judgements. It was a very low point for me. It actually still makes my heart hurt just thinking about it. It hurts, not just because people were watching with their jaws wide open, but because my son felt that fleeing the scene was his only option.

Usually, after these tantrums, my hair is in seventeen different places (including fistfuls in my son's hand), my body is dripping with sweat from the sheer physicality of it all, my breathing is loud and heavy, and my spirit is dead. Truth is, you can't make a nine-year-old be somewhere he doesn't want to be.

As I was walking back to the car, wondering where my son could be (he was probably running home, even though he didn't know the way), Bitchy McBitcherson called from the bleachers, "Giving up, huh? We can't let them win!"

She was so lucky I was too tired to turn around and flip shit on her. I was too tired of everything. But honestly, what would I say? "Hey, lady, you have no idea what I am going through on a daily basis. You have no clue, so shut the f*ck up!" I don't think that would have made me feel better. Wait, it would have for a second, but then I would have felt guilty and bitchy.

Truth is, Mrs. McBitcherson doesn't know, and will never know, what "special moms" go through every day. She won't "get it" until it is her daughter, sister, cousin, or friend that is raising a child with invisible needs. She'll get it then because they will teach her. She's not trying to be a dick; she just doesn't know any better.

It's not just strangers who judge us. I have a great friend who has three kids, one girl and two boys. I can't count the number of times she has tried to give me "advice" on how to discipline my son.

"I can get him to put his seatbelt on. I can get him to get off screen. You need to be tough. He knows I mean business and that I will not accept his messing around."

I tried to explain that he is always better behaved for people other than his mom. It has never mattered. It is my poor parenting, not my child's neurological disorders, that is the problem. I am never a good enough mother, and my children are never as well behaved, courteous, or quiet as her children are. I want to hate her, and I did, secretly, for a while. But she is my friend, and I know she loves me. She was trying to help me in the only way she knew how. Even knowing that, I still wanted to punch her in the face for it!

James is diagnosed with autism and his tantrums can still get the best of me. I know, mentally, what I am supposed to do in the midst of them. I know the right words and the right voice to use during them. I sometimes rock it and make it all better. But other times, a lot of times, I fail. I forget that I am supposed to "slow think" and remember how far he has come. I forget to be grateful that I am his mom. I forget that no one else matters but my family.

Instead, I still feel those beady eyes on me and die a little inside. Feeling judged by your peers, whether you have a kid with special needs or not, feels like shit. So, for the love of God, STOP STARING AT ME, BITCHES!

Dear Loved Ones,

Please, shut the f*ck up. Unless we specifically ask you, don't try to help us with your "expert" advice. Don't say anything to us except,

"What do you need?"

"You are the best mother in the entire world"

"You are so beautiful and look so young!"

"Can I watch the kids for you tomorrow?"

Stop judging us for what we say and do with our children. They are *our* children. We have done, and will continue to do, what is best for them. Stop staring at us and start helping us!

I don't know what goes on behind your closed door, and you don't know what's behind mine. So, let's be kind and gentle toward each other. Life is too damn hard as it is. Why make it harder?

If someone standing next to you makes a comment about my parenting, tell them about how hard I work and how amazing my kids are. Tell them how kind and powerful I am as a mother. Or tell them to shut the hell up, whichever works for you! I may not hear you stick up for me and my child right then, but I will eventually hear it through the grapevine… and I will be forever grateful and feel your love and compassion.

Thank you.

EXHAUSTED BY 8:30 AM

I recently turned forty and took stock of what was staring back at me in the mirror. My ass is jiggly and my face is old. You can't have your ass AND your face go at the same time… That's just too much reality at once! I am trying to keep my weight at least in the twenty-five pound range of what it was last year. I am not asking for miracles, but I wouldn't mind not gaining weight just by breathing. It can be exhausting having to worry about my appearance on top of everything else!

My alarm goes off at 5:15 AM to exercise, while the rest of my family is still in dreamland (lucky bastards). I do this because I get to catch up with my girlfriends at the gym, while getting my ass handed to me by the instructor. By "catching up with girlfriends", I mean, bitching and complaining about our husbands and children. Don't act like you don't do that with your friends. Is my husband fantastic? Yes. Does he help me with the kids? Yes. Does he do the dishes and the laundry sometimes? Yes. That, in NO WAY, means that I can't hate him on any given day, just for being male!

It is interesting to me that most women I know who exercise do it in the early morning hours. It's not because we love to get up when it is still dark out. It's because that's the only time of the day we can do something "for ourselves" without inconveniencing anyone else. To be clear, I don't feel like exercise is something I do "for myself". I actually hate it, and I'm pissed that I have to do it. I resent feeling I have to be a certain weight to look "good". I hate that I fall into this trap, even though I am a grown woman and know better. I know I should be happy with myself... blah, blah, blah. But such is life.

I need to get my work out done before 6:30 in the morning because I am in charge of waking up, pushing, pulling, and begging my two middle schoolers to go to school. I feed my seemingly paralyzed children. They must be numb from the waist down since they can't get off their butts to make their own cereal or frozen pancakes, or to find any article of clothing to wear at all. I "help" them pack their lunches: "No, you cannot pack four bags of Doritos and call that lunch." Lastly, I make them run to the bus stop with seconds to spare. Success! Yay, me! That was exhausting.

My two little ones are now coming down the stairs. "Mom, I need shorts! Mom, can you do my hair? I don't want the crust on my toast!" It's go-go-go until their morning routine is done and I drop them off at school. It is 8:30 AM. I AM EXHAUSTED.

I would kill for a nap, but instead, I jump in the shower to stop smelling like a skunk from my workout three hours ago. I clean(ish) the house, run errands, take kids to different therapies and doctor appointments during school hours, and then try to do some work that I actually get paid to do. Before I know it, it is 3 PM. I AM EXHAUSTED!

My crew comes barreling back into the door from school. I am conducting the afternoon schedule like a maestro at the orchestra (except my hair is greasy, and I may or may not smell like poop from cleaning up my dog's diarrhea earlier). I make sure they eat a snack, do their homework, and get their chores completed, all the while trying to rein in the tornado of crazy—that is backpacks, shoes, and underwear (yes, underwear)—that has taken over my foyer.

"Who's where with the what now? You need what signed? Picture day was today? Who smells like BO?"

God, it feels like midnight. As they are fighting over the Xbox, I am yelling at them to get outside and see the light of day. "The sun. Remember the sun?" I AM EXHAUSTED!

I start to make dinner. I don't even know why I do this "dinner dance", since not one of my children will actually eat the meal I prepare. My children, with their specific requests, sensory issues, and lack of appetite (from their stimulant medications) refuse to eat any of it. At which point, I say, "I made dinner. If you want something different, make it yourself!" Cut to: cinnamon toast and cereal for four kids. Mother of the Year, folks. Have I mentioned that I want to just lie on the couch for a minute... please, God, just one minute. I AM EXHAUSTED!

Now, it's "Activity Time". "Get ready for practice, everybody! Dad is going to drive by the house, and you have to jump into the moving vehicle to get to baseball, basketball, dance, theater, art, football, video gaming camp (seriously?) on time."

I'll take the youngest to swimming and have Coach Michael bring him home. Noemi's mom can take Ann to Girl Scouts, and Tricia's mom can drop her home afterwards, while I take John to his baseball practice. I try to quickly clean the kitchen before they get back. Oh, here they come: my smelly, dirty kids.

"Get in the shower! Brush your teeth! Put on your
PJ's! It is bedtime!" I AM EXHAUSTED!

After fighting with them to lie in bed (their OWN bed) and at least PRETEND to be asleep, I wash my face (with seventy-seven face creams and moisturizers so I don't get six more wrinkles while I sleep), put my PJ's on, set the alarm for my morning workout and lie in bed to read. Nine times out of ten, I fall dead asleep three words in.

"Oh wait, did I forget to feed the dog? Did I sign that
permission slip? Screw it, I AM EXHAUSTED!"

Dear Loved Ones,

We look tired because we ARE tired! It doesn't feel great when you tell us, "Poor thing, you look exhausted." It just makes us feel ugly.

Raising children with invisible special needs is hard work! So, want to help us out? Take the kids OUT of the house so we can actually lie down in our own beds for a little bit. Better yet, have them sleepover, so our brains get a break for twenty-four consecutive hours. It may seem weird, but sometimes a break for us could be you taking the kids out so we can straighten up the house and catch up on laundry in peace and quiet. It sounds strange, but it feels glorious to be able to watch a TV show that is not animated while we fold the clean clothes that have been piling up for weeks.

One of my favorite things to do when I am alone in my house is to straighten up, put Norah Jones on, light a candle, sit on my couch, and enjoy the calm. Getting a babysitter is helpful, but not when we just want to be in our own home. So, when you offer to come over and babysit, while we take a nap, it isn't actually helping us. Inevitably, the children will sniff us out, bang on our locked bedroom door, and never let us be in the quiet we so desperately need.

So, take our angels anywhere, everywhere…

Please, just take them.

Thank You.

SEX, SERIOUSLY?

This comes straight after the chapter on exhaustion for a reason. "ARE YOU SERIOUS? I am not kidding— are you really serious?" That's the question that so often comes out of my mouth when my husband gives me the "look". You know this look. It's the "Let's do this" look. Or the "It's been so long, and you know it" look. Don't get me wrong, I like sex. I really do. But more than sleep? Nah.

With four kids, two dogs, and our crazy schedules, my husband and I try to make a date to "be together". Actually, it is less making a date than it is negotiating a contract. Most nights, I am in bed at 8 PM, with at least one child snuggled up next to me. (By snuggled, I mean, a child is suffocating me with arms and legs everywhere.) So, nights are out. Mornings are filled with the hubbub I described in the last chapter. So, we have gotten to the point where, in order to be together, my husband needs to go into work late. But not Mondays, because I just blew out my hair. It can't be Tuesday or Thursday because I volunteer at the school. Wednesdays, I am too tired from my last two morning workouts.

Needless to say, sex is not on the forefront of my mind... ever. My hubs doesn't believe me when I tell him that other women feel this exact same way. I try to explain it is one of the main subjects a lot of women talk about when they get together. But he thinks it is just me. He truly believes that every other man he knows is getting sex every day and he, sadly, got a dud.

Don't get me wrong: Sex with my husband is great while it is happening, and I always wonder why we don't do it more often. But then life starts up again, and I forget that part. I also forget how close I feel to him afterwards. I just tend to like him more, ya know? However, sex isn't the only way to be intimate with each other.

My sexy daydream: My hubs lies next to me in bed at 8 PM, lovingly telling me what a great job I am doing with the kids and as his wife. While I am reading my book in my sweatpants, fuzzy socks and a charcoal face mask on, he's complimenting me, not because he is trying to get in my pants, but because he means it and wants nothing in return. Then we chat about our lives, making silly jokes and giggling with each other. I fall asleep with a smile on my face because I love my husband. That, to me, is intimacy and damn sexy.

Is that so bad? How come that NEVER happens? How come, instead, I am negotiating how long sex will take before we even start kissing? In my mind, it's just ONE more person who needs something from me. One more person to take, take, take. I wish, just for once, I could pee, poop, change a tampon, take a shower, or shave my legs without an audience. I am too tired: mentally, physically, and emotionally to do one more thing. Even if that one thing will give me pleasure. I'm just stretched too thin. I cannot do One. More. Thing.

I love my husband, but sex is a luxury that ends up last on the list of necessities I have to take care of each day. Sad, I know. But so very true. Sorry, honey. I feel like a bad wife when we haven't had sex in a while. It becomes one more thing to make me feel bad about myself. I start to tell myself that I can't make anyone happy. I tell myself I SHOULD be having sex twice a week in sexy lingerie. What is wrong with me? Why can't I be a better wife? This self-hate talk adds to my poor self-esteem and makes me feel unworthy of my husband's love.

It is not a fun place to be.

Dear Loved Ones,

This isn't just about sex. It is about everyone taking from us. What about our needs? You can help by not adding to our plate. Please don't ask me to make my famous dessert, which you know takes at least three hours, for your BBQ. Don't ask me to come over and set up your Netflix account because you don't know how. Watch a YouTube video on how to do it. Don't make me feel guilty that I am not volunteering as homeroom mom.

Please don't ask me what my kids want for their birthday or Christmas presents. This is my biggest pet peeve! Don't ask me to not only think of a gift for you to get my kid, but then pick it up, buy it, AND wrap it. Shop for yourselves… I have my own gifts to buy! Do you seriously think I have enough time and energy to think about what YOU should be getting my children? I am grasping at straws as it is trying to come up with my own ideas. Figure it out on your own. I know you can do it! I have faith that you can find something for a nine-year-old girl's birthday all by yourself. And if you can't? Cash. You can always give cash.

Low self-esteem is common among moms raising special kids. Most of the time, no one is telling us they love us for all the things we do for them. It is usually the opposite. Kids, husbands, family and friends are more apt to tell us what we didn't do, what we forgot, or what we missed than appreciate all of the many things we did right! We keep trying to do right by everyone but continually feel like we are missing the mark, whether it be not having enough sex with our husbands, not putting in enough volunteer hours at the school, or backing out of plans with a friend for the second time in a month. We are never going to be perfect so help us to stop striving for it. Remind us that no one you know is having sex twice a week, and that we are all in the same boat. Keep reminding us that we are perfect the way we are.

Thank you.

UNITED FRONT

As a treat, I recently took the kids to an indoor water park. My youngest and I were patiently waiting in line for a small water slide. I was feeling as proud as punch that day because, not only was James enjoying the water, he was not screaming about the way his feet felt on the wet cement. I remember thinking, "I am killing it today!"

Cut to: a boy, about eight years old charges up the steps, butting in front of everyone, ignoring the lifeguard, and happily jumps right on the slide, screaming in delight the entire way down. My automatic thought is that this boy probably has some underlying issues he is dealing with. I go to that assumption immediately because I believe most humans are dealing with issues, but also because neurotypical eight-year-olds usually know to wait their turn. I think nothing of it and continue to wait in line with my son.

There are two moms in front of me, each with one kid. They start asking aloud, "Where are the parents of that child? Who raises their kid like that? Isn't that just

disrespectful? I bet his parents don't discipline him for it."
Yadda, yadda, yadda.

I am standing there, thinking, "You IDIOTS.
Obviously, the parents of that child are having a rough day.
Obviously, those parents need some compassion." Maybe
I just have my "Spidey special needs sense" that makes this
clear to me and not the other moms.

The lifeguard tells the women that the boy is here
often and has autism. Without missing a beat, "Oh, well,
that is still dangerous. He could have hurt another child.
He should have a wristband or something so everyone
knows that he has autism. Besides, if he does have autism,
his parents should be on top of him even more."

I am silently arguing with myself at this point,
trying to decide whether I should say something to these
women or let it go. I want to tell them that they are the
reason people like me, a mother with a special needs child,
feel like shit all the time. I want to suggest *they* wear a
wristband, so everyone knows they are bitches. I am
debating whether or not to say, "Give him and his parents
a break! As a parent with a child who has autism, I beg of
you to shut the f*ck up. Take your daughter down the slide
and just shut the f*ck up! We don't need your advice,
bitches; we need you to shut your pie hole. Why can't you
just smile at the happiness that kid just experienced on that
slide, morons?"

My feelings are so strong about this because I feel
guilty. I failed that boy and his parents that day at the
waterpark. I should have said those things to those women
aloud—for all the moms and dads who live our life. But I
said nothing. I didn't want to cause a scene or have a

confrontation. To the mom and dad of that darling boy, I am so sorry that I didn't shut those women up. I will do better next time, I promise. And sadly, there will be a next time. In the meantime, I will always let your son or daughter budge in front of me.... every darn time.

That's the good part about our invisible special needs community: There are parents who get you, really GET YOU. I am thankful to the parents who have seen my children doing something that screams ADHD, autism, or sensory processing disorder and quietly prayed for them or given them a smile. I don't always see it, and the kids would never think to tell me about it, but I know you did it.

The reason I know is because we are a team, a united front, that stands up for our special needs kids. I am proud to be a part of the united front that is "Parents with children who have invisible special needs". I promise, from now on, to have you and your child's backs.

Suck that, ladies in line at the slide. I learned a lesson from your ignorance and will speak up from now on.

Dear Loved Ones,

Please don't judge any child for any action he/she does, or for what they are wearing or eating. They are just that—children.

Just say a quick prayer for them and their parents. Do better than I did and stick up for the kid everyone is putting down. Be our backup. You don't have to curse like I would have.

Help us to educate those who are ignorant about invisible special needs. If you see or hear someone say something negative to my child, you have my permission to BEAT SOME ASS. Or, at the very least, tell them to shut up!

Thank you.

TO LABEL OR NOT TO LABEL, THAT IS THE QUESTION

I have to be quite honest: I don't understand the controversy surrounding being open about a child's diagnosis. Why is the word "labeling" even a thing? To me, it's pretty simple: my kid has autism, my kid has ADHD, my kid has anxiety. My kid has autism, ADHD, sensory processing disorder, anxiety, AND fine motor delay... Why would anyone, other than those who want to support him, even care? I mean, really?

If I am honest and tell the school my son has these issues, they will evaluate him to see what, if any, special education is needed. The staff will put him with a teacher who is really good at being strict and on-point with her schedule. If I am honest to the insurance companies, they will pay for his medication and therapies with zero out of pocket from me. Why wouldn't I tell everyone? Who cares? Why would anyone else care if my kid has these issues? What is the downside of being "labeled"?

Some argue that being labeled doesn't give their child a fair shot at being seen as a "regular" kid. The truth is, usually, your kid will never be seen as "regular". It's just how it goes. Others argue that what their family is going through is private, and they don't want anyone to judge them or their child. I can understand that. I guess it goes back to me not caring about what other people think of me.

At an open house for middle school, I walked up to Joseph's new guidance counselor. I introduced myself and asked to schedule a meeting to discuss what might or might not occur during the school year with my son, and how we could keep our eyes on the prize (my darling Joseph). If being "labeled" gets my kid the resources he needs, then be my guest: Label away!

On a selfish note, I tell everyone that I have four kids, most of whom have invisible special needs. I WANT you to know that I am working my f*cking ass off! I am tired, beat up, and just trying to put one foot in front of the other. I want you to see my struggles and think, "That girl's awesome." So, I don't want just my kids to be labeled; I want it, too!

People are so afraid of being "labeled" or "outed" for fear of others noticing that they are not perfect. I tell the hilarious story about how one of my kids drew penises all over his math test and the call from the principal that followed. Later, away from the group, a mom will tell me her daughter has ADHD and that they have been struggling for a year now. Another mom will tell me her son has autism, and she knows exactly what I am talking about.

I have been at this bus stop with these women for

four years now. Four years! Why have they been so quiet about their kids' issues? Is it because it is none of my business? That is certainly true, and I completely understand. Or is it because they don't want anyone to know they are human with human problems? That poor woman has spent the past year struggling with her daughter alone and in hiding. That sounds horrible to me! It may be none of my business, but if I know about it, I will support you. I will give you names and numbers of people you could contact to look into x, y, or z. I will hug you on a day that sucked. Why so quiet, everybody? Who are you hiding from?

In my mind, the more people I tell, the more people who can support me. Maybe I believe in people too much. Maybe my vision of everyone supporting each other and not judging one another is too lofty. In real life, people are assholes, and it can be hard to put yourself out there for all the world to see. Luckily for me, I hate assholes and am going to do my best to not care what they think. Instead, I will embrace the support and love I get from everybody else.

Dear Loved Ones,

Embrace my child's diagnosis! Yell it from the rooftops in a happy, proud way.

Don't whisper the words "autism", "ADHD" or "anxiety", when talking about my kid. Tell everyone you know that your grandson has autism and is the coolest kid in the universe! Tell your kids that their cousin has anxiety but still went on that roller coaster and KILLED IT. Be proud of my child for succeeding in life because of his disorder, not despite it.

Each time you brag about my child, my heart swells. Don't tell me about the severely autistic child at the mall and how lucky I am that my son isn't "that bad". Look at each child. Really, look at them. They are more than their diagnosis.

Love them for who they are and celebrate us!
Thank you.

SPEECH THERAPY, OCCUPATIONAL THERAPY, PHYSICAL THERAPY... OH, MY!

Something people who don't have children with special needs may not know is that coordinating insurance, doctors' appointments, therapies, and medications is, in fact, a FULL-TIME JOB. I have spent countless hours on the phone with insurance companies, filling out paperwork, fighting for appointments to be pushed up, and taking kids to evaluations. It takes an enormous amount of energy to fight for the right therapies to be given to your child and then work to get them covered by insurance. Moms who are working outside the home AND working with insurance, appointments, and therapies deserve our highest praise. You are awesome! I am so impressed by your energy and determination to get it done. You go, girl!

For some reason, there is a covert society with insurance secrets that some moms know and newcomers into this world don't. I had absolutely no idea about insurance before my sons were diagnosed with ADHD, autism, and anxiety. I didn't even know what a deductible was. I was embarrassed by my ignorance of what was and wasn't covered under our plan.

I bumped into a friend of mine while chaperoning an elementary school dance (another wild and crazy Friday night for me). She made an off-the-cuff comment about how her son went to the dentist because he chipped a tooth and, "Thank God that he is on Medical Assistance for his ADHD, so it was free."

SAY WHAT NOW?!?!?! I'M SORRY, DID YOU SAY "FREE"?!?!?!

I peppered her with questions and found out I had a lot to learn about insurance. I spent weeks, if not months, learning the rules, ways, and regulations of all different types of insurance. You have your main insurance and your secondary insurance. You have some doctors that take that secondary insurance but some who don't. The application for Medical Assistance needed so much information that it felt like I was giving away my first-born child for free healthcare. Depending on the day, it would have been an easy trade! After all that work, the application came back denied because they said they didn't receive certain paperwork. So, I sent it again. Another rejection. What I learned is that the second rejection is to make me want to give up and stop trying (I'm talking real shady shit). I sent it the third time. I guess they realized I wasn't going anywhere, and lo and behold, my son was approved!

SCORE! BOOM! TAKE THAT, BITCHES! Someone once told me it's the mama bear who doesn't give up that gets that insurance. Boom, baby, boom! So, with that insurance, EVERYTHING my son needs medically is FREE. Occupational therapy, physical therapy... free! Break his arm... free! Dental work... free! Many people don't know about this. Look into it. It is worth every sweat and tear.

The next tasks that took years off my life were the evaluations. OMG, the evaluations. James was evaluated a million different times for every different service he could potentially receive. At one point, he was wearing a swim cap connected with a ton of wires and listening to the ugliest sounds I have ever heard while watching different lights on a screen. The poor kid was trying to pull off the cap because it was itchy. As he was crying, the technicians were yelling at him to not touch the wires! Apparently, this cap costs a buttload of money. It got to the point where I felt so bad that he was always being "tested" that I took him to his favorite water park, Great Wolf Lodge, as a reward. No person should have to endure all that, let alone a four-year-old.

After the evaluations, appointments had to be made for all these wonderful supports he could receive. So, once a week, every week, he would go to one occupational therapist to learn how to put on his clothes while regulating his sensory input. Another occupational therapist would work on his fine motor skills. Then he would have two hours with the behavioral therapist for Applied Behavioral Analysis. He would also take a swim class to get a break from living in an overloaded sensory state. Don't forget I would have to "brush" him three times a day to help his sensory issues. That is exactly what it sounds like. I rub the brush across his skin, and the pressure input targets touch receptors and helps him organize his central nervous system. His siblings would make obstacle courses around the house to get his proprioceptive input, his awareness of limbs, in line. He also needed to see a psychologist weekly, whom we referred to as the "talking doctor" for his anxiety.

My heart would break to see this poor boy working so hard, being pushed to his limits every day, all day, so he could reach certain goals. What made it even harder is that he couldn't even understand why he needed to do all of this. It must have seemed to him like we were trying to "fix" him. Like he was not Ok just being himself. It still makes me sad to think of it like that. On the other hand, thanks to all those amazing therapies, he is in class with his peers and is learning to manage his specific challenges, just like every other kid in the class!

Now, imagine doing that for more than one child. Now, imagine doing all of this and working outside the home. Craziness! This shit is hard-core and no joke. It is not something you should or could do alone.

Dear Loved Ones,

Please know we are stretched so thin. All these appointments and therapies are even harder to juggle when we have more than one child. Want to help us? Offer to pick up the other kids and take them to their activities. Offer to watch the kids, so we can have a "date" with one of our other children, who may be getting less attention than they need. Go to the softball game that we can't make and cheer the loudest for #7. That is so helpful! Do what my mother did for me: take all the insurance bills that were incorrectly billed, call the insurance companies, and take care of it for us. That job was going to take me months to finish.

Don't make me ask for help. Offer it. Anytime you are taking your kids to the movies, Chuck E. Cheese, or bowling, offer to take one of ours with you. Our children need those outings so much, but we can't give those experiences to them at this time. There is only one of us, and as much as we would like, we cannot do it all. It would be really easy for you to pick up one of my kids to go with you.

We aren't just worried about our "special needs" kid; we are up nights worried about the effects this is having on our other children as well. Take our preteen to the movies and watch something that isn't rated G.

We feel guilty that we can't do it all.

Thank you.

SENSORY ISSUES ARE MORE THAN JUST AN ITCHY TAG

Anyone blessed with a cutie who has sensory issues knows this scene: the screaming, crying, and yelling over pants, socks, T-shirts, buttons, gloves, hats, tags... It is horrible for both child and parent.

Before James was diagnosed with Sensory Processing Disorder, I didn't know anything about such things as proprioceptive and vestibular output. I learned later from his occupational therapist that proprioception and the vestibular system are the awareness of one's body in the environment and one's balance and movement. What I did know was that something wasn't right with my son's outbursts about clothes. James was three years old, and getting him dressed was hell on earth. Any piece of clothing we put on him was wrong. More times than not, he would end up in the car in complete hysterics, with only his Superman undies on. I can't tell you the number of times I dropped him off at preschool in this non-outfit because I didn't have it in me that morning to do the dance.

What I thought was my boy being a tough nut, a very "spirited" child, or one determined jerk was actually something serious.

As a tradition, my husband and I take the kids to the Philadelphia Thanksgiving Day Parade every year. We have it down, man. We bring the wagon, fill it with Dunkin' Donuts munchkins and hot chocolate, blankets, tiny chairs for each child… We are ready. The Thanksgiving James was three years old, my eyes were opened. It was a HUGE turning point for our family. HUGE.

So, here's the story: Getting four kids into their snow gear on that particular snowy and cold Thanksgiving Day was an event within itself. But my husband and I were on it. Three kids were dressed and ready to go. Next up, James. Ok, PJ pants first. Easy-peasy. Next up, snow pants. I tried and tried and tried again. He was fighting, kicking, and screaming. I was sweating my ass off. I was definitely not feeling very thankful at that Thanksgiving Day moment. I finally out-maneuvered him, got his pants on, and buckled him in his car seat (confinement via five-point harness, thanks be to God). Success! I chucked the clothes I didn't get on him—his sweatshirt, hat, gloves, winter coat, socks, and shoes—in the back of the car, and we peeled out of our driveway like a bat out of hell.

"We will have fun at this parade, damn it!"

As we drove the thirty-five minutes into the city, James never stopped screaming. I'm not talking about whining or normal crying but screaming as if his legs were on fire. Screaming as if he were being tortured.

I started crying and yelled at my husband, "This

isn't natural! Something is wrong! Something is really wrong! Pull over!"

He pulled over on the highway's shoulder, and I took James' snow pants off. He immediately stopped crying. For the rest of our ride, my poor kid just did that sad hiccupping thing that happens after a really bad cry. I told my husband that I would be calling the doctor on Monday. My mommy instinct was set off, BIG time.

I called the pediatrician and told him what happened. I expected him to have us come in immediately, where he would order an MRI, CAT scan, and blood tests—stat. Instead, he told me it was "a sensory thing" and that he didn't really believe in it. If I wanted to look further into it, I could, "...try TheraPlay or someplace like that. Some kids just don't like the way socks feel. I had to deal with it with my daughter until she grew out of it. He will grow out of it, too."

That didn't cut it for me. I could still hear my baby's screaming in my head. This was more than just an uncomfortable itchy tag. Instead, I had him evaluated at TheraPlay. They told me he needed occupational therapy for sensory issues and oh, by the way, he has fine motor delays as well. "None of his teachers ever said anything to you about that?"

I said his preschool teacher told me he had trouble holding scissors, "But he's a boy and still so young that he will pick it up sooner or later."

At his first occupational therapy appointment at TheraPlay (where I paid hundreds of dollars out of pocket because I had not yet learned about Medical Assistance), the therapist told me that James' screaming episode was

100% real and he most likely felt like he had "spiders and bugs crawling all up and down his legs."

WHAT?!?! She explained sensory processing disorder to me. I was devastated that my poor baby had to deal with this, and I had no idea what he had been going through this whole time.

She said, "Imagine how bad you would scream if there were creepy crawlies all over your legs."

I'd flip the freak out, lady. I would literally FLIP THE FREAK OUT.

From that day forward, we did all sorts of things to teach James how to manage his sensory input and output. I never "made" him wear something that he refused to put on again. I learned to listen and trust my three-year-old to know what his sensory needs were. Actually, that was the first step on the long journey to his autism diagnosis. Snow pants are what made us look more closely at our youngest son's behaviors.

That was the beginning of my long career fighting for answers and advocating for him. That was how Early Intervention started for my young son.

So, after that Thanksgiving Day episode, you can imagine what my kids are dressed like at any given time. At church, John, who also suffers with sensory issues, wears PJ pants. He pretty much wears PJ pants every day. Thank God, PJ's are "kind of" cool in middle school. James is barefoot everywhere we go: rain, snow, sleet, or sun. You should have seen the stares when we were in Disney World and my then four-year-old was walking around barefoot. Was it gross to me? Absolutely! Was he hurting anyone? No. Ok then.

Sensory issues can go beyond clothes. John will gag at the smell of yogurt. His brothers and sister think it is hysterical to run around the house after him waving a Go-GURT. It is a pretty creative way to torture your sibling! James must smell EVERYTHING. He will pick up and smell every cookie on the plate until he finds the perfect one for him. Sorry, germaphobes... that's my kid. Deal with it.

On that same Disney World trip, James picked up a dirty flip-flop, smelled it, and I swear, in slow motion, I watched him take it to his mouth and lick it. HE LICKED THE BOTTOM OF A DIRTY FLIP-FLOP. What am I supposed to do with that? I mean, besides throw up a little bit in my mouth. Oh, dear Lord, his immune system must be rock f*cking solid.

Imagine my fear when John was about to have his First Holy Communion. A suit? You want my son, who doesn't take off his pajama pants, to wear a suit and tie? And dress shoes? I was so worried, I called up his doctor and asked him if he could prescribe John a Xanax (and an extra one for me) for his big day. I had no idea how Holy Communion was going to go down. I spoke with the director of his religion class and explained our predicament. What was she supposed to say? "Sure, he can wear his feety pajamas as he accepts the Lord, Our God, in his most precious state, and it will be totally fine. No one will even notice?"

For the record, his doctor refused the Xanax... for both of us. My husband and I had John "practice" wearing the suit for one minute at a time for weeks before his Communion. The morning of the biggest Sacrament of my son's life, I felt physically sick at the thought of him being tortured in his suit. I mean, we did all that we could as parents; the rest was up to him.

God held both our hands that morning. John looked so good in his suit—better than any other kid there, because I knew how hard it was for him. He did it! I am tearing up right now at the memory of that feeling I had in my heart: pride, joy, and a sense of being blessed. I felt like we could take on the world. He could do anything because we would work so hard together to get him there. That day felt like a miracle. But it wasn't a miracle; it was John kicking ass and taking names as he put into practice the occupational therapy techniques he had learned.

At any holiday kindergarten concert, it is so easy for me to pick out which kids have sensory issues and are trying their darndest to make it through without losing their shit. Some kids make it work, and others break down crying. Those teary-eyed kids are the ones I want to whisk off the stage, smush their little cheeks together and tell them they NEVER have to do something that makes them feel bad again. I want to tell their parents about occupational therapy for sensory issues and that their child could be feeling legit pain. I want to hand out noise-cancelling headphones at fireworks every 4th of July. I want to take every kid who is struggling with some invisible pain or discomfort and envelope them in understanding and love.

I wish it were that easy. I wish I could tell who all these kids are, but sometimes we will never know. Invisible needs, am I right?

Dear Loved Ones,

Please try to refrain from making comments about my child's fashion choices. It may have taken him hours to find the perfect shirt and pants that don't make him feel itchy and yucky. Those hours that he was trying to find said shirt and pants entailed torturous talks and negotiations over every article of clothing he owns. When you see my son in an outrageously inappropriate outfit for an event, give him props for his own personal style and sticking to it. Make him feel good about himself, please!

If my son is wearing noise-cancelling headphones, don't make the Something About Mary reference, "Have you theen my batheball?" It's not funny, even if my son doesn't get it, because I do.

Most of the children you see are being raised the best that their parents can raise them. Trust that odd clothing is not because that child is not loved but because he IS loved, and those parents are choosing to let their children be comfortable.

Don't judge. It's just that simple. At the kindergarten graduation, lean over and tell me that my kid's your favorite because he rocks his own look and only sings the songs he wants to. Tell me you admire his resolve. Thank you.

PLEASE DON'T LEAVE ME!

The divorce rate for couples who are parenting a special needs child is staggering and scary. Russell Barkley, the ADHD guru, cited that couples raising children with ADHD are three times more likely to separate or divorce than couples who don't have a child with ADHD. So, I thought we should discuss divorce. It is a sad reality and definitely not uncommon.

Some couples are in a marriage where they hold hands, stare lovingly into each other's eyes, and validate each other's every thought and feeling. Good on them. I'm jealous. Other couples hardly see each other because they work a "divide and conquer" plan. I hear that. Some couples might be in therapy, trying to figure things out, while other couples might be staying together for the kids or finances. Some couples will never even contemplate divorce, while others dream about it or are in the midst of it right now.

Actually, my husband and I have been ALL of those couples at different points in our lives!

I don't need to tell you marriage is hard. F*cking hard. Now, add kids. Now add ADHD, autism, anxiety, sensory processing disorder, and (add your issue here). Even f*cking harder.

It makes total sense to me that couples can't make it work. I mean, the woman my husband married sixteen years ago is pretty much dead. The woman I am today is the complete opposite of who he chose to love for the rest of his life. I used to be competitive and athletic (the qualities that most attracted my husband to me). Now, no competition is worth my mental energy and my once powerful body that could take me through the finish line of an ultra-marathon is now riddled with sciatic nerve pain and arthritis. I used to be fun. Now, I am in bed at 8 PM (7 PM, if I am being honest).

For the record, my husband hasn't changed much at all... not his foundation. He is balder and maybe a bit crankier, but that's it. He really hasn't changed at his core. He also didn't grow children in his body and give birth to another human being. I believe that's where it all changed for me. My entire perspective has changed in the last fifteen years of raising our kiddos. My entire compass has been shifted. I feel bad for my husband, a bit. Sorry, pal, you got duped. It was an unintentional bait-and-switch. My bad! I had no idea this was going to happen. In fact, if we were to go on a first date tonight, he might not ask for a second. Maybe I wouldn't accept it anyway.

Parenting is hard. Parenting with someone who has different views or beliefs to you? Super hard. No matter what the issue:

Should our son HAVE to keep going to football

practice if he hates it and his anxiety hits the roof? My dear husband says yes, and I say no.

Should we bring our child to church, knowing all he will do is scream and yell for the entire hour? My husband says yes, and I say no.

He says up, and I say down. We used to be on the same page about many things; now we're not even in the same book! Almost EVERY stance and view I took and agreed with him on is now the complete opposite.

He goes to work every morning, and I sometimes wonder why he comes home at night. Especially in the beginning, when we were up to our eyeballs in autism and ADHD with no clue what the hell was going on. Pretty much the second he walked in the door, I was throwing him a child and saying, "He's all yours." I was explaining to him which child was a nightmare all day and which kid is never leaving their room again. I gave him a list of my grievances before he even put his work bag down. I now understand how annoying that must have been for him. Sorry, honey, but such is life. I feel bad for him sometimes, and then I remember that he pooped in private at work today, and then I don't feel badly for him anymore. I haven't pooped in private in fifteen years.

Our life is messy and ugly and beautiful and crazy. So far, my husband and I have been doing a good job of not killing each other. (Yay, us!) Some couples chose to part ways and co-parent, and some are still on the fence either way. And all of this is Ok. It is not a success or failure. These parents are doing what they feel is best for their family. We all are. Whether a couple stays together or not, everyone knows that co-parenting special needs children is ridiculously hard. No judgements here.

There was a period when I was scared my husband was going to leave me. Why wouldn't he? Our life sucked. I often dreamt of driving away and never coming back but knew, in my heart, that wasn't a real option for me. But men have left for much less than raising a houseful of ADHD and autistic children. I am sure he dreamt about leaving, too.

My fear wasn't just that he would leave ME. It was that he would leave me WITH THEM. I used to panic at the idea of not having anyone to hand them over to at 6:30 PM. He hasn't left us yet, and for that I am grateful. I know that makes me sound pathetic and desperate. Truth is, when parenting our kids, I am both of those things at times.

Dear Loved Ones,

Divorce does not make us quitters. We did not give up too easily. We tried and tried and tried again to make it work. We love our children and want what is best for them. Please do not lecture us on the disadvantages of children growing up in a "broken home". In fact, please don't use the words, "broken home". We know all of it, and we feel sick about it. Don't make us feel bad about something that already makes us feel like shit.

Tell us you are sorry it didn't pan out for us, but you know we tried our best to make it work. Tell us that our kids are resilient and that they will endure. Reassure us that we are not being selfish or ruining our children's lives. Trust that we are doing the best we can. Pick us up off the bathroom floor, buy us a pair of Spanx, and teach us what dating looks like these days. Tell us we deserve romance, passion, and to be treated like a queen! Be with us every step of the way on the new journey we are about to face. Because we are scared to death.

If we are miserable in our marriage, and you see us struggling, pray for us. Hold our hand. Assure us that no matter what we choose, to stay or go, you will be there for us.

If you don't agree with whatever decision we make as a couple for our family, keep it to yourself! You do not get to tell us you are disappointed or believe we are wrong. We don't need that. In fact, it might just push us over the edge.

Just love us. Support us. Be there for us.
Thank you.

IS THAT A SHARPIE?

The "half glass full" person I am thinks ADHD keeps our lives full of fun. Most days, when my angels do something less than stellar, I laugh about it because otherwise I would cry. My kids, with their ADHD and autism, keep us on our toes and can even make us giggle at the awkwardly funny and crazy things they say and do. It's not the worst thing ever to see one of them peeing in the backyard at a friend's BBQ. It isn't horrible to have my kid come down the staircase of a friend's house, wearing her underwear all over his body as he shouts, "Here comes Captain Underpants!" Sometimes, I can see the humor in it. No harm no foul.

The things I lose my mind, and my temper, over are when one of them has ruined someone's property. In fact, nail polish is my nemesis. My youngest son and I end up at little girls' houses often because we take my daughter to her playdates. I will stay for a cup of coffee, start chatting, take my eyes off the prize—James—and relax. Wrong move, Mom. Wrong move! He will sniff out that little nail polish, open the lid, and proceed to "paint" the furniture, rugs, beds, and floors of that poor girl's room. Nail polish doesn't come off certain things, people. What do I do in these situations (yes, plural)? I throw my coffee mug on the counter, apologize profusely, grab him, and run out the door. There are nail polish stains in little girls' homes throughout our neighborhood. After a couple of years of this, I started to get annoyed at the parents for keeping it out! (Not fair but true.)

One day, my girlfriend was picking James up for a T-ball game. As I was helping him buckle up, I noticed a Sharpie on the passenger seat of her minivan. My eyes bugged out of my head. "Is that a SHARPIE? In your car?"

She casually said she must have left it there from the other day. WHAT?!?!?! Can you guess what my Honda Odyssey would look like if I, accidentally, left a Sharpie in it? Ruined. Ruined! My car would be ruined.

I took the Sharpie from her seat and asked, "You can just have this here and your kids won't draw on the car?" She gasped, "Of course not! They know I would kill them!"

Ummm… yeah. My kids know I would kill them, too, but I would still have butts and curse words drawn all over the leather interior!

It's not always big things like Sharpies and nail polish. James will find the one thing another child cherishes and, without meaning to, ruin it. Color on it, break it, rip it. Again, he is not trying to be mean; he just does these things without any thought to that toy's owner. The number of apologies I have uttered cannot be counted. The number of times I have felt like crawling into a hole and dying of embarrassment cannot be calculated. That favorite sweater of Grammy's? Slime is now embedded in its fabric. Yep. My sister's new Coach purse? Gatorade is now in a puddle at the bottom of it. Yep.

I feel like a failure when that stuff happens. In my mind, I can hear you thinking that I can't keep my children under control. Truth is, I can't. Not if I want to have a conversation or, God forbid, a cup of coffee. I have to be 100% on all the time. It's when I am sipping that coffee with a friend, thinking, "Life isn't so hard," that he strikes, and I am furious at myself for not knowing better. It isn't my child's fault—it's mine. That may sound like an excuse, but it is my job to teach him right from wrong, and in those instances, I wasn't there to do that. I know better than to relax and let my guard down. Shame on me.

This is one of those times I can have a major pity party for myself. I don't get to sit around and talk with other moms as our kids play. I have to follow my little guy around and intercept the fist he is about to throw at the little boy who is playing with the red car. He wants the red car. I need to see three steps ahead of my son, so I can catch him before he makes a poor choice and teach him the better option. So, no chatting for me. At these affairs, I end up leaving early because I see no point in being there. It is just a reminder that my life is different to the other moms' lives. I will drive home, silently crying, feeling bad for myself. Then have a cup of coffee alone. The pity party tends to end after my caffeine boost and my son's request to play UNO with me. Then I can laugh and see how sweet my boy is and feel how much I love him and wouldn't change a thing. He is mine and I love him.

Dear Loved Ones,

How about one huge blanket apology?

I am sorry for anything that my family has ruined—and will ruin at some point in the future. We feel like complete shit when this happens.

This is a lot to ask of you, but can you pretend that sweater that just got cut up wasn't expensive? Can you pretend that the figurine that just got knocked off the table and broke was not a family heirloom?

In these instances, please tell us not to worry about it (and then curse us when we leave). We feel so horrible as it is. To see your visible disappointment will put us in a depression for at least a week.

It is a lot to ask, I know, but we need this. And maybe, next time we come, move your valuables so I am not sweating the entire visit.

Thank you.

THE PARTY HE WASN'T INVITED TO

After reading about how Sharpies and nail polish ruin my life, you won't be surprised to hear that, due to those types of incidences, my son wasn't invited to many playdates or birthday parties during his preschool years. I don't blame those other moms. I wouldn't want my house ruined either. At three years old, he had no clue he was excluded. However, having my middle school kid not invited to a party that will be posted all over Facebook brings out my "Mama Bear" attitude. It makes me want to cut a bitch.

My eldest son, Joseph, eloped from school in his first year of middle school, and it was a huge deal. He couldn't handle school anymore and just decided he was done. Fortunately, the principal isn't a fan of not having all the kids accounted for (thank God), so it led to a bit of a scene. Word got around school, and kids were talking about him. Rumors spread that he got arrested, was expelled from school, and was going to "juvie". Some of his buddies stopped texting him to hang out. He was confused, but I saw the writing on the wall: their parents didn't want their kids hanging around my son. Ouch. Seriously, ouch.

Let me set the record straight, for his sake, and say all those rumors were false.

A year later, he still didn't have a huge social group. He had one good friend. The following year, he made another poor choice at school and stopped hearing from that friend as well. The problem with having only one friend is that one wrong move, and you are down to zero.

What do I want to say to the parents of these friends who told their kids to stay away from mine? I understand that you don't want your child hanging out with the wrong crowd. Neither do I. My son is a middle school boy who made a mistake. It's as simple as that. I get that until your child makes a mistake like that, you may never have the compassion to see past my kid's errors. Joseph is not setting fires, bullying kids, or hurting animals... He walked out of school once and made a smart-ass comment to the teacher another time (and he was punished for both transgressions by us, trust me).

Give him a break. Give me a break. Let your son hang with mine. I promise he won't corrupt him... at least, no more than the other boys would. The mama bear in me wants to say, "He has ADHD, a neurological disorder, you jackass. He is doing the goddamn best he can! Help a brother out, man. He's a good boy!"

In the meantime, those same moms will wave to me across the parking lot or give me air kisses and tell me we should grab a coffee sometime. And I will accept all of it with a smile because guess what? Her kid is going to make a mistake, too. It's not a question of if, but when. And I will have compassion for her (after I say to myself, "How's it feel, bitch?"). I will let my son continue to play with hers because we are all human and we all make mistakes. I don't think any mother wants to see any child sad. Whether someone has a disability or not, when a child hurts, his/her mom hurts double.

Dear Loved Ones,

The emotional upset of our children completely trumps every sad emotion we have ever had for ourselves.

We may call and tell you about how our son was teased, left out, or pushed. We will cry to you that he was the only kid not invited to a party. Be angry for him—and for me.

Tell us that those kids are assholes and don't deserve "our boy". Tell us that those mothers who would allow their kids to not include him were never cool and you never thought they were pretty anyway. Tell us, "We don't need them. We have your back."

Tell our kid that he is super cool. Have your kids be nice to mine.

Being supported is an awesome feeling. It makes us feel less alone. Your support reminds us that our children are good people and don't deserve to be left out.

And on the day of the party that our kid isn't invited to, invite him out and do something totally awesome with him.

Thank you.

FOR THE LOVE OF GOD, PLEASE LEAVE!

Remember that divorce rate I mentioned earlier? I have to say, I get it. Forget what I said about fearing my husband would leave me. Now, I am begging him to get the hell out! Here's your hat, what's your hurry?

Look, husbands can be REALLY dumb. God love my husband, but in what world is it Ok to walk through the door from an eight or nine-hour workday and head straight to the bathroom for forty-five minutes? We both know you are pooping for the first five minutes, and the other forty minutes you're reading Sports Illustrated or trolling Facebook. You ass, I'm not stupid! I also know that you conveniently ask the kids to play catch with you outside immediately after dinner, so I am stuck doing the dishes. Well played, sir. But most women know these tricks. We know you can be morons. I am not saying wives aren't morons too. But let's focus on husbands right now.

My friend's husband once came home from work

and immediately went to the bedroom to lie down. She asked him what he was doing, and he said, "I'm tired."

She replied something along the lines of, "Exsqueeze me? You are tired? You are an ass… I'm tired, too! I didn't realize we could just go to bed. If I knew that, I wouldn't even get up in the morning. Get your butt out of that bed before I kill you with my bare hands!"

Like I said, morons.

Most wives complain about their husbands, but "special moms" have more ammo than most. After Joseph was diagnosed and we became educated about his disorders, my husband was still having a hard time understanding why his kid acted the way he did. I could explain ADHD to my dear husband until I was blue in the face, but he still couldn't get it. When James flushed ninety-six Legos down the toilet and broke it for the third time, my hubs still yelled, "What were you thinking?" even though he was taught that our son can't answer that question, because he truly doesn't know the answer.

"Why would you do that? What's the matter with you? Why can't you get this? Why is this so hard for you?" These are all questions most fathers have yelled at their frontal-lobe-challenged kids. I have told Nick one hundred times that these questions are not helpful to our child. I have been saying this for at least ten years, and yet he just said it again as I am writing this. Do you know how many battles have been fought over this? It may actually be easier to count the glasses of wine I've had in the past year: Nah, both are way too many to count!

Sometimes it feels like it would be easier to raise the kids by myself. Sometimes. It's easier now, but earlier, on days that were really bad, and we were in the eye of a storm, I couldn't wait for my husband to come through the door and rescue me. Other days, I would wish he would turn right back around, get in his car, and go somewhere else. My days with the kids were so unpredictable that there was no way of knowing if my husband would make things better or worse. That was a stinky situation for both of us. Neither of us knew if I would love him or hate him that day.

Looking back at that point in our marriage, I feel bad for us. We had no idea what we were doing or how we were supposed to make our "special needs family" thrive. We were so young when this all started. I am thankful that we made it out of that turbulent time. I know we will have many more battles to contend with along our journey, but all we can do is tackle one at a time. All we can do is try our best and ask God to hold our hands during those times.

As much as he drives me insane and can't, for the life of him, remember to give the kids a warning before he turns off the TV (inducing a huge meltdown when the screen just goes black in the middle of their favorite video), my husband shows up every day with love in his heart, and ultimately, that's all that matters.

On days when I want to kick him to the curb, I have to remind myself that his good intentions and kind heart are why we have made it this far.

Dear Loved Ones,

Let us vent about our stupid husbands. Let us tell you how bad he messed up and how hugely frustrating he can be. However, after we spew our hatred, don't tell us to leave him. Don't talk badly about him. Also, don't negate our complaints by telling us what a great guy he is. Just close your mouth and open your ears.

To be clear, in most cases, we KNOW our husband is a good guy. He is actually a GREAT guy, but don't interrupt our rant! We need you to have a short memory because we are going to let go of whatever dumb thing he did today, and we need you to never bring it up again. It's like complaining about my mother: I can do it, but you can't.

So, let us complain about our spouses. Then, the next day, let us tell you what a great dad he is without so much as a hint of remembering yesterday's conversation. Because co-parenting a special needs child or children is extremely difficult!
Thank you.

TAKING TO THE BED

Everyone has their own way of escaping from their lives now and then. I have friends who have a hard day at work and need a glass of wine to reset. I have another friend who curls up on the couch, watches mindless TV, and eats an entire family pack of Oreos. We all need an escape from time to time. Some people do the healthy thing and go to the gym or journal their feelings. Not me. When a day kicks my ass—and by "day", I mean my beautiful family—I "take to the bed". It's the phrase my husband and I coined because I literally put on my PJ's, wash my face, and get into my bed... whether it is 12 PM, 3 PM, or 6 PM.

Some days, I just have to call it. They have beaten me down. I give up. You win, I lose. I'm out. Thank you and good night.

This happens to me more often than I care to admit. The reasons, in detail, are different, but the theme is the same. Being a mom of children with ADHD, autism, anxiety, sensory processing disorder, and ODD can really suck ass. Some days, I rock it, and other days, I fail terribly. But, unlike having a bad day at the office, I didn't fail my boss; I failed my child. Disappointing a boss can never feel as bad as the pain associated with disappointing your child. There are days when I feel badly for my kids because I missed something that another mom probably wouldn't have missed.

For years, John was so sick with the symptoms of ADHD and anxiety, and I didn't know it. To be honest, I thought he was just cold or emotionally dead inside. He wore a hoodie every day and didn't participate in life. He didn't say, "I love you," or kiss me or let me hug him for two years. TWO YEARS! Imagine being a mother and not hearing "I love you" or getting a kiss from your child. Can you imagine the pain my heart felt? Those were some of my worst days. My son was so distant, and I didn't know how, why, or what to do about it. He used to be my cuddle bunny. I was failing him. I knew it and felt helpless and hopeless.

I brought his symptoms up to our pediatrician and said I thought he might have autism. She dismissed me fairly quickly, and so I never brought it up again. She would know; she's the expert, right? Years later, AFTER James was diagnosed, I learned everything I could about ADHD, anxiety, sensory processing disorder, and autism. I realized John did suffer from these things and could have benefitted from all the therapies James was getting in Early Intervention. I blew it. I screwed him. I let John, for YEARS, feel broken, alone, sad, different, and uncomfortable in his own skin. I can still "take to the bed" if I think about that too hard. So, failing as a mother is a bad day, times ten.

I have "taken to the bed" for many different reasons:

- After a violent tantrum, when I am in physical pain from restraining one of the kids to keep him and his siblings safe.
- For being in complete and utter confusion about how my kid could act in such a way.
- When one of the kids gets in trouble at school for something big, like threatening a teacher or handing in a test blank, just because he can.
- When we are sitting in the church pew behind a family whose kids are praying reverently, and my kids are dressed like slobs and acting like assholes.
- When someone makes a negative comment about my child, that suggests his behavior is due to my parenting skills.
- After an argument with my husband over how to handle our screaming, oppositional, aggressive child.
- Just out of pure exhaustion from this life.

"Taking to the bed" is really a description for my pity party. I can lie in bed, give up, and feel bad about the hand I have been dealt. "Why me? Why can't anything be easy? Why can't I get a break? Why didn't I stand up for my son when that mom corrected him? Why was I embarrassed that my kid was playing by himself at school? How bad am I screwing up his life? Will this ever be Ok?

Will I ever get it right? I give up. This life is too hard. Let me just lie in bed and pretend I am invisible."

This may seem dramatic, but I truly feel this way sometimes. Most women with kids with invisible special needs believe the stakes are so high that failure will ruin a person: *their* person. One too many missteps by me, and my kid could be a pregnant teen or a drug addict. If I missed his occupational therapy this week, he could be behind on learning to manage his sensory overload. It's not a report that can be fixed, or an Excel spreadsheet that can be tweaked. It's our children. And it is ALL ON US. That heavy weight is on Mom. Always. It gets tiring and overwhelming.

You know what helps me though? Taking to the bed or drinking a glass of wine while listening to Norah Jones. Ya know what else helps? Encouragement and kind words. My dad is awesome at this. He will often tell me I am a great mom. He will constantly tell me that I am amazing for being able to keep everything together (even when it is obvious I haven't brushed my hair in a while).

If I am organizing the kids' seven trillion medications, he will say, "Jeez, Julie, you are amazing to know all that." He will say, "I don't know how you do it, but you are one terrific mom." Or, "Julie, you work so hard for your kids to be happy, and I can tell it is working."

Those words can get me through a day, a week, a month. They can help me persevere through the tantrums, inflexibility, and the emotional dysregulation. It makes me remember and feel proud that these kids are mine. God gave them to ME because He knows I will love them and do everything in my power to help them. Words like those make a difference.

So, whether you are the wine drinker, the emotional binge eater, or the sleeper, it's cool. No judgment here. You do what you need to do. Honestly, we all need and deserve a little pity party now and then. So, go for it.

Dear Loved Ones,

Please be the encouraging voice we hear. Tell us all the good things we are doing as moms. We are our own worst critics. Help us change our inner dialogue by inundating us with positivity and love. Your words can make—or break—us.

We are fragile. We may look like mama bears who can do anything, but we need to hear that we are doing a good job as much as possible. Trust me, it will never get old.

Tell us you are proud of us: THAT really helps. Tell us how lucky our kids are for having US as parents. It feels good to be appreciated. It feels damn good to be noticed for this thankless job. We don't get a paycheck or an "atta boy" from our boss. There is no raise or promotion to validate our hard work.

Your words are all we have. Give your compliments loud and often.

Thank you.

SPRING BREAK? CHRISTMAS VACATION? SUMMER? OH GOD, PLEASE NO!

My sister works for a school and like every kid and teacher, counts down the days until summer vacation. She works full-time outside the home and raises three super-cool kids. She loves and NEEDS spring break, winter break, and summertime. Her family needs time to be together and get a break from the daily stresses of school and all that comes with it. No packing lunches, rushing to pick up or drop off, or homework to check. My sister gets a chance to breathe on those days when they can get up when they want, fart around all day, and just chill out.

My view on any break from school is the complete opposite. I am a stay-at-home mom, and the hours from 8:30–3 PM are my heaven on earth. Heaven. On. Earth.

So, to know that my days during breaks and summer will soon be inundated with kids 24/7 is as scary as shit to me. Now, add kids with invisible special needs. So, can you see how these breaks may be something that I dread?

Three weeks before spring or winter break, I begin to have anxiety attacks as I try to figure out how to entertain my children. I need to have activities planned, so the fighting over screens twenty-four hours a day for a straight week will not kill me. I start preparing for summer in the month of April. The number of brain cells I have lost figuring out a way to make our family time together peaceful, happy, and calm is immeasurable.

My two anxious kids who live and die by a schedule, start to act out about a week or two before a break. They can smell a change of routine in the air like I can smell a homemade brownie being baked by my neighbor. James will have meltdowns over things he hasn't been upset about in months. He knows what's coming... uncertainty. To make things go smoothly, I set up schedules and daily activities to keep us as close to "normal" as possible.

But ya know what isn't fun for breaks and summers? Having every second of your vacation planned down to the hour. My house does not have the same chill vibe that my sister's house has on a break. I wish it could. I can handle being on a tight schedule during breaks, but it can suck for my two kids who don't have issues with flexibility. I am in a catch 22: make two kids feel calm and comfortable or make the other two kids feel confined and trapped. And the right answer is... your guess is as good as mine. To make our time together bearable, I lean to the scheduling side.

Don't ask us to go on a last-minute trip anywhere.

Don't ask us to change our plans for the zoo to meet you down at the shore for the day. That invitation sounds awesome to four out of six of us, but it ain't gonna happen. Just writing that bums me out. I LOVE an impromptu gathering. I haven't had an impromptu anything since my darlings' diagnoses. I am not blaming them... or am I?

I hate to admit that I may be blaming them, but at this second, picturing us on the beach for the day, I feel resentful. I am mourning all the fun, spur-of-the-moment trips we never get to go on. Shit, now I have to take to the bed!

James' therapist recommended to us that the kids be enrolled in six weeks of day camp to keep their schedule and routine as constant as possible, putting their minds more at ease. So, here I am: not bringing in any money as a stay-at-home mom but paying for camps. Unfortunately, my kids don't understand or feel they need the benefits of the routine that camp gives them. So, every morning, they tell me what a horrible mom I am because I am shipping them off to the worst place ever: summer camp. I am the WORST MOTHER EVER.

BTW, just for clarification: I would love to go to summer camp right now. Just sayin': hang out with my friends for six hours while people entertain me all day? Sounds f*cking great to me. But no. In my children's eyes, I am the devil.

So, there is an asterisk next to summer camp in our world. The last few summers have been very hard for me as a mom. James would refuse to get out of the car to walk into camp. When he wouldn't walk in on his own, I would have to chase him from the back of the car to the front of the car, trying to get hold of him so I could carry/drag him to the entrance. I was Ok with this physicality because five to ten minutes after I left him, he would go on to have a great, fun day. So, as I was dragging him inside, the counselors (who were all of sixteen years old) would stare at me. Just sit there and stare at me. In the beginning, I would kindly ask them to take/rip him from me as I ran out of the door. By the middle of the summer, I would be yelling, "You just have to grab him!" By the end of camp, they stopped helping all together. I understood. They were teenagers getting paid bubkis. This was, by no means, in their job description. I am sure that, at some point, the director told them they shouldn't be grabbing or dragging kids ever! No hard feelings. I mean, no hard feelings NOW. Last summer, when I was in need, oh, I had hard feelings. But I get it.

Let me give you a quick mental picture of what I would look like after camp drop off: I would have scratches on my face, my hair would be in twenty different directions, my shirt would be scrunched up revealing my extremely pale belly that is covered in stretch marks and loose skin. My breathing was loud and labored, and I would be sweating like a pig. Every. Morning. For. Six. Weeks.

I knew what "the judgers" were saying behind my back because I could literally hear their whispers. People should really work on their whisper volume. "He obviously shouldn't be going to camp. She needs to stop torturing him. Why would she put him through this? Doesn't she stay home?"

Others would say things to my face like, "He must just need special mommy time. Poor thing."

Shut the f*ck up, people! Do you think I do this because I enjoy being a sweaty-ass pig drenched in sweat, sadness, and guilt? Ugh. I do it because the "experts" tell me it will help my child in the long run.

Truth is, most mornings, I would drive home crying. Shit, I am crying right now thinking about that drive home! I believed, beyond a shadow of a doubt, that I was the worst mom in the world and was ruining my son. But I kept taking him because that is what the behavioral therapist and doctors told me to do. They told me this would help him. It just didn't always feel that way.

So, THIS summer I am trying something different. I am going to send James to a summer camp made just for kids with invisible special needs! Why did I not do this sooner, you ask? Well, two weeks of this specialty camp is the price of six weeks of our regular camp. Two weeks of this camp is so much money, I had to talk myself into hitting the "submit" button about eight times before I could pay the tuition. My baby is worth every penny, but what about the other weeks in the summer? My husband and I decided we wanted to spend our money on this camp. We are blessed that we could send him at all. So, we will tighten the budget somewhere else. I can only pray that this is better than the other camps. I am getting older and don't know how much more pulling/dragging I can do. Something's got to give.

This camp that cost a million dollars? One month before it's due to start, the director of Camp Pegasus called me and recommended that, since James has a hard time transitioning out of the car and walking into the big entrance, we meet her on the side of the building at a quiet, smaller door, where he can walk right in and head straight to the sensory room. Huh?!?!?! Um, hell yeah! That's why they get paid the big bucks. The fact that this woman can already understand what my daily morning struggle entails is reassuring. I already feel like they "get" him. And they "get" me. At this stage in the game, to me, being understood is priceless.

When I see a child begging, screaming, and fighting to not go somewhere or do something, I start praying immediately for that mom. I have been that woman. I am that woman. Unfortunately, she doesn't know I have been in her shoes. She thinks she's alone on the island of misfits. And that sucks.

For moms with kids with invisible special needs, summer is not "easy breezy". In fact, it can f*cking stink.

Dear Loved Ones,

Summer is tough.

Want to help? Offer to take the kids down to the shore for the weekend. THAT would be amazing! Offer to take the kids out for the day. Just take them somewhere, anywhere! Do you have a son/daughter who is old enough to babysit? Have them babysit for four hours, three times a week for us. Have it count for their service hours. What a great way to teach compassion and kindness! If we could grocery shop alone? Ahh, you have no idea how amazing that feels.

If you see a woman struggling with her child in the midst of a tantrum, assume she is doing the best she can. Go over to her and say, "My (grandchild, cousin, friend) has tantrums like this. How can I help you?"

She may say, "No thanks," or she may ask you to close the minivan door behind her as she wrestles her child into the cart. Either way, she will feel your genuine concern.

We need to feel like you "get" us or, at least, want to try to.

Thank you.

MOMS RAISING SPECIAL NEEDS CHILDREN ARE ALLOWED TO BE FAT

I am going to spend the rest of my life getting a law passed by Congress that states: "If you have a child with special needs, you are allowed, nay, encouraged to be fat. You are also encouraged to grow out your gray hair and your upper lip mustache. Legs and armpits, too. Hairy and proud."

That's what we deserve. Give us a break, for God's sake!!! You want us to be superhero parents, AND you want us to look good? SHAME ON YOU. SHAME. ON. YOU.

Don't we, as mothers of kids with special needs, deserve some sort of benefit? (Yes, beside the benefit of raising beautiful, lovely children... blah, blah, blah). I think the benefit should be that we get to eat an obscene number of Oreos—in peace. We should be applauded for our extra weight. Think of all the emotional eating we do because our kids stress us the hell out!

So, let's go, ladies. We can do this. Let's march upon the Capital and demand that we get this law passed. The fact that I am expected to be skinny, pretty, have zero cellulite, and wear heels, WHILE taking care of my kids with ADHD, autism, and anxiety is just mean. MEAN.

If there were a law that we didn't have to shave our legs anymore, I wouldn't feel bad when I throw shorts on and realize too late that my legs could be mistaken for a monkey's. Or I wouldn't feel bad when I am not wearing makeup and bump into Bitsy and Mitsy in the grocery store. They would actually say to each other, "Oh, God love her, she looks like shit… That's how good a mother she is!" They would be at the next PTA meeting telling everyone that they bumped into Julie Falcone, and she looked SO BAD that she must be acing it as a mom.

Don't worry, ladies, after I write this book, lawmaking will be next on my list. You are welcome ahead of time. Let's start eating the Oreos now, to get a head start!

Dear Loved Ones,

Never mention our physical appearance, unless you are going to tell us how great we look. Do not tell us we look tired or that the bags under our eyes show we haven't been sleeping. Just say nothing.

Hold your tongue before you give us a backhanded compliment, like, "You look good considering..." or "Poor thing, you look exhausted." These are not cool.

For birthdays and holidays, do not get us something for exercise. No thanks to the DVD or the weights or the membership to Curves. Just steer clear of that entire thought process!

This is very important: If you ever mention our weight, there is a chance you will be killed. Don't say I didn't warn you. Trust me.

Thank you.

THE PERKS OF HAVING A KID WITH SPECIAL NEEDS

There are perks of having a child with special needs. I mean, beside the main ones like: we have the best kids on the planet, hands-on learning about compassion, patience, empathy and all the other bennies we know in our hearts.

There are other perks, too, ya know? And I am not above using these perks whenever I can. I mean, what's the point of having to deal with the negatives if we don't get the positives?

We get to budge to the front of the line at amusement parks because our kids can't stand and wait in long-ass lines without acting like wild animals and going postal on everyone's asses. Thanks for that, James!

We have an automatic excuse to leave any dinner, party, family gathering, or holiday we don't feel like being at. "Sorry, my son is about to explode. I am going to get him home. Sorry, he's just had too much stimulation today.

I best get him home in a quiet and dark room. Gotta go, the babysitter is having a rough time with my son; I need to relieve her. I know, it sucks. Sorry to rush out." It's the perfect escape hatch! Thanks, John!

We have the benefit of requesting what teacher we want, the kids we want in his class, and where we want him to sit. We get these benefits because we know what our child needs better than anyone else. So, the teacher who gives a buttload of homework is out, and the teacher who gives out Hershey's Kisses when her students wear their "smiling faces" to the classroom is in! The kid in middle school that pushes our kid's buttons cannot be in the same class as ours, but the boy with the amazing manners can sit next to him at lunch for the year. Thanks, Joseph!

We get out of certain duties. I'll take it! "Oh Julie, I don't know how you do it. You have so much on your plate. Don't even think about coming early to set up for the school dance or staying late to clean up". "Having four kids is hard enough, but with all their issues? God Bless You!" Thanks, kids!

At church, when they are all behaving like animals and our family looks like one hot, crazy mess, we get a pass because, "What great parents to take their kids to church even though it is difficult."

For the most part, the teachers and principals tend to be a bit more understanding when your kid flips the bird at another kid or impulsively says, "Screw you," to his teacher. (BTW, I just heard about that; I wouldn't know that from experience.)

Your support group is more likely to grant you a night out or a weekend away with your husband because,

"You two work so hard. You need special time together."
Thanks!

Once my new law is passed, we get to be fat and let ourselves go!

My favorite benefit: family and friends love my kids a little extra. My friend, Karen, makes it her mission to get a hug from James every time she sees him (not in a creepy way, I promise). And when she gets one, she makes a huge deal about it, and my heart feels so warm and tingly. My other friend, Amy, has John over for playdates all the time and will tell me how cute her son and mine are together. She will tell me how sweet he is. It's the reminder I need sometimes, and it makes me feel great. When the kids do ANYTHING cute, sweet, or good, their grandparents will brag to everyone who will listen about their young grandson who just, "Called out the lady in the grocery store for budging to the front of the checkout line. That woman wasn't expecting a nine-year-old to put her in her place! Isn't he a hoot?"

These are some of the perks to having a child with special needs. Thank you, children!

Dear Loved Ones,

Don't be jealous that we get these awesome benefits. Our kids have it pretty tough on a daily basis, so if they get to budge to the front of the line at a carnival, happily move aside, please.

I know you will find it unfair that we get to be fat without being shamed, while you have to count calories and run marathons. But it will be the law, so deal with it. Thank you.

SCHEDULES, SCHEDULES, SCHEDULES

If you were to walk into my kitchen right now, you would notice that every cabinet, inside and out, has routines and schedules taped to it. These lists help my kids with ADHD, autism, and anxiety stay on task. They need to actually see and study the routine. Structure and consistency help my anxiety guy feel like he has more control over things. The lists help my son with ADHD have something to reference when he forgets what he is supposed to be doing. And for my autism cutie, it brings him comfort to know what is coming next.

"What kind of schedules, you ask?" Let's see: there's your run of the mill Morning Routine, Afternoon Routine, and Bedtime Routine. If one of the kids can't think of anything to occupy themselves, they can read the "Bored?" list, which has different activity ideas for them to consider. We have your Daily Schedule, your Screen Schedule, your Chore Chart, and the token economy chart, which rewards positive behaviors with tokens that can be exchanged for goodies. Don't forget the Tally chart we needed to make because one of our angels had to work to pay for a broken door caused by his fist. Some of these haven't been used in years but are still hanging up just in case, God forbid, we need them again.

Now, don't get me wrong: I love a good schedule. I, personally, like to write my to-do list the night before, so I can be productive first thing the next morning. I like to write lists, and then lists of my lists (usually because I lose the original list at some point throughout the day).

I also don't mind a good routine. That being said, the numerous procedures surrounding my family can be a bit much to take in, even for me.

When someone outside my ADHD, autism, and anxiety bubble walks into my home, they are mesmerized. They will look from one schedule to the next, staring as if I am the best/most neurotic mom in the world. I have had many women say, "I wish I could be this organized," or ask, "Can I take a picture of this chore chart for my house?" I usually reply with, "Oh yeah, we are BIG schedule people."

What I am not saying aloud is that these schedules aren't hanging up because I Pinterest too much (which I do) but because without them, my house would be UTTER CHAOS. I am not talking a little messy. I mean my children would be running around in circles, very likely naked, bumping into each other, not knowing what to do or how to do it. Without these schedules, my kids would be on some sort of screen device for eight straight hours, making them zombies who end up being a teary mess by bedtime. Schedules for my crew are a necessity!

James cares about his schedule only so he can figure out when he will get his iPad.

"What do I have to do to get my iPad?"

"Let's check the list." It totally works for me when he gets his homework done, eats a snack, and finishes his chores without a tantrum. That's a win. Other moms see my charts as organization; I see them as survival.

It doesn't always work the way I plan, however. Here's the problem: I like a schedule, but I don't NEED a schedule. So, often times, I set the chart aside because I CAN remember what needs to be done next. That's when we fall right back into the tantrums, arguments, and struggles. I end up wondering what the hell happened. It is a vicious cycle. I forget that these charts are my children's oxygen. I get used to us all being on point, then I forget that the reason we are working well is because we are keeping to the routines. And then we have to start back at square one. In fact, there was a time when James would do anything not to go to school. I would have to hold him down in the car, so he wouldn't jump out. We realized, with the help of his therapist, that we were getting lax on his morning schedule and he couldn't handle it. My bad.

My family needs schedules and routines to be successful. So, if you go to Wegman's Grocery Store at 3 PM, any Monday afternoon, to get the fried chicken dinner, like we do EVERY week, you'll bump into us! If your child happens to wear green socks on a Thursday, our kids could be twinsies, because Thursdays are ALWAYS green sock day! Nothing like a good routine to keep us in line!

The negative to this regimented life is that

spontaneity is dead. There is no cheering when I offer to take us to Bingo Night on Friday evening because that's Pizza Night. Duh, Mom! I am NOT the hero when I surprise my son, at his school, with his favorite McDonald's lunch. Instead, I am met with irritation: "Mom! You know I eat turkey and cheese on Tuesdays. Ugh!"

I try to deny that this monotony is my life. So, I do something spontaneous, like taking a dreaded Happy Meal to school, and end up getting kicked in the ass for it. That always snaps me back into reality! I mean, who doesn't want a f*cking Happy Meal? I would kill for a chocolate milkshake from Mickey D's right now! But alas, McDonald's is only acceptable after a soccer game. Sigh.

Dear Loved Ones,

These charts, lists, and routines we make are for a reason.

We are not trying to be neurotic freaks (that's just who we have become). Don't scoff, or shrug off, the "militant way" we keep to the schedule. I promise you, we are trying to keep the kids calm. So, when you see our schedules or tasks that need to be done, just smile and tell us what wonderful moms we are, instead of calling us, "whack jobs who are too organized."

When you are babysitting for us (thank you, by the way), keep to the schedule and routine we have provided. It is not that we don't trust you or want to micromanage you; we are looking out for you and our kids. Just follow the schedule to the T, without any lip.

We know what we are doing. There is, in fact, a method to our madness. It helps all of us in the long run. Trust us. You don't want to deal with my child in the midst of a tantrum because you wouldn't give him his snack in the correct bowl.

Thank you.

FAKEBOOK, I MEAN FACEBOOK

"Julie, I had NO idea you were going through that! You seem like you have it all together."

I wish, when someone said that to me, I could take it as a compliment. But I don't. That makes me feel like an imposter. If I look like I have it all together, then I am not putting my true self forward. I do not have anything together, and most days I am hanging on by a thread. In the beginning of our invisible special needs journey, I cried ALL the time. I never want another mother who is walking this journey with her special needs child to ever think that she should have it all together. In fact, I encourage her to be a hot mess for as long as she needs. For me, each day is different. Today I am having a good day. Tomorrow, I'll be knocked on my ass.

I have decided that I HATE Facebook. I say that, but still scroll down and look at my feed constantly. I mean, is it EVER going to feel good to see your old classmate having their new house built from scratch on three acres of land? Is it EVER going to feel good to see a girl you hated in high school engaged with a huge rock on her finger? How about the family picture with the skinny mom, handsome dad, and the three kids in bow ties and suspenders? You have NEVER seen my children in suspenders, and if you did, someone must have had a gun to their head. Actually, that's not true. They would rather die than wear those things. My point is… it's all bullshit. We know it, and we *still* fall for it.

The money for that brand-new house your classmate is having built is from the malpractice suit she won from her botched vaginal rejuvenation surgery. The girl with the huge rock? She married for money, not love. And the family picture? That's easy. Those kids were forced to dress like that and were miserable that entire photo shoot. Oh, and that handsome husband has the hairiest back! Ahhh, I feel better already, don't you?

Fake is not me. It doesn't serve anybody to fake it (insert your own sex joke here). Let's be honest: I am a hot mess, as are my kids and husband. Even my dog is depressed. Most of my friends are hot messes, too. Face it, so are you. So, if you want to flaunt your new vacation home or your new Louis Vuitton shoes, go for it. But we all know the truth: you cry too.

Don't misunderstand me: I don't begrudge anyone wanting or having nice things. Nor do I want anyone to cry or be unhappy. I LOVE when my friends, siblings, nieces and nephews are succeeding at life. Luke got a promotion! Nathan hit the game winning homerun! Hope got into Harvard! Jordan got the lead in the school play! Will made captain of the hockey team! I am genuinely happy for each and every one of them. In fact, we will be the family in the front row of the play and the loudest fans at the baseball game. They celebrate our successes too!

It's not that I don't want everyone to experience happiness, I just want us to also be encouraged to commiserate together about the hairy backs, sad state of our vajay-jays, and less-than-stellar parts of our lives, as well.

So, let's band together, don our sweatpants and fuzzy socks, and post pics of us being human and real. Like a picture of my kid with nail polish all over his body because I tried to read a magazine alone. Post a pic of something REAL and stop pretending life is perfect.

With all this hashtag business, we should make one ourselves.

#FuckBeingFake
#InvisibleSpecialNeeds
#ICrySometimes
#LifeCanBeHard
#IDontHaveItAllTogether
#ILoveMyKidsButTheyAreKillingMe
#StopStaringAtMeBitches

What's your hashtag? Let your freak flag fly. I got your back!

I learned that the more "real" I am, the more people want to hang out with me. No one wants to hang out with "perfect" people. We want to associate with women who have to hold their vagina when they sneeze, too. Discussing the benefits of Botox with other wrinkly women, is far better than with the non-wrinkly women

133

who deny getting it. The moral of this story is to stop bragging and be honest. If you had an unfortunate incident while getting your hiney hole waxed, tell me about it and I'll be over with a casserole in one hand and a bag of ice in the other. But, constantly brag to me about your daughter winning the award for "Best Person Ever" (which you assure me is a real thing) and expect less casseroles and more eye rolls.

Being real is the only way I can be anymore. It could be that I am just too tired to put the effort into making my life look perfect for others, or that with age comes self-awareness. I no longer care if people see my flaws. Those who love me, accept me for who I truly am and that's all that matters to me.

Dear Loved Ones,

Join us in being real. Be proud of your f*cked up friend, daughter, or sister who is living a life of chaos with her special needs family. Tell us, "Perfect is boring, and those people on Facebook are liars."

Don't point out that our sisters' kids achieved Honor Roll while you know our kids are struggling to get C's. Truth is, we are psyched they are C's and not D's. We need you to brag about our kids. Tell someone with pride that your daughter's kids are so fun and spirited that each day is an adventure and makes you smile! Brag that your grandchildren are keeping you young and you love every minute of it!

Want to show us your new Chanel bag? Go for it! Maybe you could gift us your old one considering we can't afford to buy something nice when chances are high that our sweethearts will ruin it. We aren't shelling out top dollar for a t-shirt from Abercrombie and Fitch that our sensory-sensitive kid might find too "itchy". However, we wouldn't mind experimenting with your child's hand-me-downs!

Thank you.

IS THAT A HOLE IN YOUR SHIRT?

I am going to admit something I am super-duper embarrassed about. I am literally cringing as I write this because I don't want you to think less of me.

Before I had my kids, I 100% judged a special needs mom. There. I said it.

Ugh, God, I hate myself. I was celebrating a family member's birthday at a nice restaurant. My cousin was there. She is the sweetest person on earth. Truly she is. At this time, she was in the midst of taking care of her beautiful son, who had a lot going on health-wise. This mama bear did everything for her son, who couldn't do anything for himself. Jack was awesome. He had curly hair and adorable thick glasses that made me smile every time I saw him. He was God's beautiful handiwork. I prayed often for him and his family. Then it happened: my disgusting thought. God, forgive me.

I saw my cousin wearing a dress that was really old

and washed out. There were holes in the collar, and it just looked... sad. I mean, we were at a party. You couldn't find anything else to wear? Really? I know you are working your ass off, but anything without a hole in it?

Hate me. Go ahead, I deserve it. You can't hate me as much as I hate myself. I am ashamed of those thoughts.

Now, let me tell you what I would think and do today if that same thing happened. First, I would hug my beautiful cousin. Hard. Then I would tell her how beautiful her child is and what an amazing job she is doing raising him. I would tell her how happy I am that she could get out of the house and have a drink or two—because she deserved it. I would ask her if there was anything I could do to help make her life easier... and I would mean it. I would see that hole in her dress and think of what that hole represents: the blood, sweat, love, and infinite tears she has shed for her child.

I am ashamed of what I thought those many years ago. The only good that I can find from that experience is that it gives me great perspective on what other people are thinking and why. Most people aren't judging us because they are mean... but because they JUST DON'T KNOW. People aren't trying to make us feel like shit all the time. They don't even know they are doing it!

I was an ass. An ignorant jerk just for thinking those things. I am sorry, cousin. I didn't know what I didn't know. And now that I do, I admire what you did for your son in the too few years he was on this earth, even more. You were the perfect mother for Jack.

I can only hope I can be half of that for my children. So, a hole isn't always just a hole. That hole represents someone's life story, which we know nothing about.

Dear Loved Ones,

Please try and understand this: you just don't know. You don't know what happened to us today or yesterday. You have no idea the struggles we have to handle, whether emotional or physical with our child.

Help us, hug us, and most importantly, try to understand us and what we are fighting every day. Have compassion for us—we are so tired and feel so down.

If you see a hole in my shirt, food crumbs in my hair, or two different shoes on my feet, see them for what they really are: exhaustion. Instead of wondering why I didn't look in the mirror before I went out, just be proud of me for getting out of the house at all. I learned my lesson for sure.

Thank you.

NOT RAIN!

My sensory-sensitive kids have so many "quirks" that can make or break any experience. For example, James will not go outside if it is raining. The way the rain feels when it hits his skin makes him feel uber uncomfortable. He hates the feeling of being wet. That can make things a bit difficult when we have to, ya know, do anything on a rainy day. Sometimes, I wake up to the sound of raindrops hitting the window and whisper to myself, "Not rain. Not today." Then I put my big girl undies on, drink an extra cup of coffee, and get ready for the struggle that is about to ensue.

Another interesting quirk we deal with is James' tolerance for pain. If he gets hurt, and we don't see it actually happen, we will never know how, when, or why the bruise that takes up his entire left butt cheek is there. We need to inspect him for bruises, cuts, or scrapes because he doesn't feel pain the same as we do. If we didn't see him run, headfirst, into the door, we would have no idea that he needs to be evaluated for a concussion. I am just waiting for Child Services to call because he will, at some point, be walking around with a broken bone for weeks before we notice.

Or, how about John's obsession with arriving early for everything? On time is late, and late is unacceptable. If we are late, it can quickly ruin our night. So, when you see us already in our seats at the elementary school strings concert an hour before the show starts, it is not because we want a front row seat (that is just a bonus). It is so my cutie doesn't flip out and ruin his sister's violin debut as he screams about us being late.

Ever see a family early for a dentist appointment? Come with us to a check-up. Even though John HATES the dentist and cries throughout the entire visit, we are still sitting in the waiting room a good thirty minutes early.

Since the school doors open at 8:40 AM, my little buddy, the unofficial school welcome wagon, likes to arrive no later than 8:30 AM. Duh!

So, that's why we do the things we do. We are not ALWAYS doing "weird" stuff like that, but when we do, I have learned not to apologize for it. If being early helps my child feel more at ease and less anxious in his own skin, consider it done.

Dear Loved Ones,

Don't question us. If you see something that may not make sense to you, like my son sledding in shorts and crocs, don't ask us what the deal is. Just bite your tongue. Trust that we know what we are doing. Trust that we haven't gone completely insane and just let us "do us". Don't automatically judge us as unfit parents. Give us a chance to earn that title! Instead, just smile at the pure joy you can see in my kid's face as he flies down the snowy hill.

We are not beating him or locking him in the basement at night. We are letting him wear what he is comfortable in, even though it is not socially acceptable. One might argue that, instead of being criticized as parents, we could in fact, be praised for the way we put our child's needs and desires before what is deemed appropriate by strangers.

I bet someone is making a trophy right now with the title, "BEST PARENTS EVER" that will be presented to my husband and me at a black-tie affair. I will have lost ten pounds and look amazing in a black ball gown, and my husband will rock a slim tuxedo. We will be interviewed by Ryan Seacrest and get invited to be on Ellen. She will offer me a job to go all over the country, surprising awesome parents with $10,000, on behalf of The Ellen Show. The segment will be called, "Amazing Parent Patrol". Feel free to let Ellen know I'm awaiting her call. Reporters, on the red carpet, will ask us how we could be so young and attractive and also such amazing parents. We will thank God and the Academy. Nick and I will be the new "it" couple.

We will change the way the world sees success. Instead of how much money is in your bank account or the size of your home, it will be parents of special needs kids who are lauded and seen as heroes. So, be good to us now, so we will remember "the little people" and let you ride on our coattails.

Thank you.

PARENTING WITH ADHD

There is a part of my family dynamic that I forgot to mention. Funnily enough, I have ADHD, too! I say "funnily", but my husband would use another word, I am sure. Maybe, "the most f*cked up part" is more accurate. After doing loads of research to learn about my kids' ADHD diagnoses, I recognized those same symptoms in myself. Chances are, if a child is diagnosed with ADHD, one of the parents has it, too. Let the blame game begin. My husband reminds me all the time that the poor mental health genes come from my side of the family!

I have fought depression most of my life, so I am very comfortable talking to therapists and being on antidepressants. I went to my psychiatrist and told him my self-diagnosis of ADHD. Unfortunately, he didn't see this as a concern. I felt like he didn't take my symptoms seriously and instead, made me feel like I was an Adderall druggie trying to score a script. I worried that he was pegging me as a stay-at-home mom who only wanted Adderall to get skinny. This doctor told me he didn't think my ADHD was a big problem since I "didn't have a job that I needed to focus on". Immediately I felt unworthy of medication because apparently, being a stay at home mom was not a job deemed important enough. I shut up, felt stupid, and forgot about it. What a shame! One YEAR later, my therapist's hypothesis was that I was clinically depressed because of my undiagnosed ADHD, which, in fact, was proven to be true.

Most of my life, I have forgotten things, missed meetings, not paid attention to small details, started something and never finished it, and just constantly dropped the ball. I thought it was a character flaw. My therapist explained that a lifetime of "messing up" sparked decades of self-hate talk, which led to depression. She believed that if I could manage my ADHD, my depression would lift. Well, Smartest. Lady. Ever! She convinced my psychiatrist to put me on a stimulant. Six months later, I was no longer clinically depressed. It has been an amazing journey.

The positive of having the same disorder as my kids is that I can better understand what they are going through. I get it. I can empathize with them about forgetting to hand in homework or getting so worked up about something and being unable to calm down. I never need to ask, "Why would you do that?" because I know why—their executive dysfunction. I can relate to them and what a blessing that has been for both me and my children. Our relationship is now based on understanding and compassion.

The negative of having the same disorder as my kids is that I mess up at parenting—a lot. Now, I have to remember to stay on top of me so I can stay on top of them. That sounds crazy. My Post-it notes are to remember my kids' Post-it notes!

There have been occasions where I have neglected to make dinner or help with homework, because I have become super-focused on my new Pinterest project. My husband has walked in at 8 PM after working late to find the house in shambles, the kids unbathed and watching TV, while I am reading a really good book that I can't put down! That night usually ends with me feeling ashamed and embarrassed at my irresponsibility.

The upside to my ADHD is that my linen closet is organized by color and material. I scrubbed all the baseboards down the other day because I saw a spider web on one of them and then just kept going until the whole house was done. I can also get into a mean game of UNO with the kids and forget to drop one of them at basketball practice or drama rehearsal because we are having so much fun together.

My poor husband. I can really exhaust him. Sorry, honey. I don't mean to be unproductive. I don't mean to forget to do the laundry six days in a row, so you have to wear a pair of boxer shorts inside out. I just find other things to do that are more interesting! Luckily, my meds have helped me, so we can now all wear clean clothes every day (or at least, confidently do the sniff test).

Parenting ADHD children while also managing your own ADHD is tricky. I will never get it all right. I am smart enough now to not expect to get everything done or done well. I try to make lists (and lists of my lists) and set alarms and timers to remember the important tasks of the day. It is just one more thing to add on to our already filled plate.

HOLY CRAP, IT'S 3:30 PM! I HAVE TO PICK UP THE KIDS FROM SCHOOL...

Dear Loved Ones,

Don't tell us that our doctor is wrong, and we do not have ADHD. We do. It is not a conspiracy made up by the pharmaceutical companies to make millions.

We will look like a hot mess most of the time. We will leave keys, coats, books, you name it at your house after we visit. We will forget we were supposed to meet you for coffee and then feel like complete f*ck ups when you call to find out where we are. We just forget. Period.

We hate this about ourselves. We are intelligent people, and it is very frustrating to come across like we are ditzy and dumb. You are allowed to make one joke at our expense when we come flying into the party an hour late, hair wet from the shower, and two different shoes on. ONE joke. After that, leave us be. We feel like an idiot already.

Help us when it comes to remembering important things. Remind us to call Aunt Doris today because it is her 80th birthday. Buy an extra Christmas gift and leave it at your house, so when we forget to buy something for Luca's new baby, you got our back. Those things will help us feel like you "get" us and love us.

Don't roll your eyes or laugh at us like we are dumb. We are most likely smarter than you; we just don't come off that way. Don't belittle us. We are putting so much energy into things that are not hard for you at all. Treat us like we are the intelligent people we are.

You don't have to understand why we struggle with seemingly easy tasks, but it would be great if you could accept and love us for who we are!
Thank you.

MOMMY GUILT

Do you have a while? The topic about a mother's guilt could keep me busy for days, weeks, even months. Every mother feels guilt about her children. "I didn't breastfeed. I ate blue cheese during my pregnancy. I didn't catch the autism symptoms early enough. I didn't let him be himself. I was too tough on him. I was checked out. I took to the bed when he needed me most."

I could go on and on.

Guilt is ugly, and it is NOT our friend.

Now, let's get more specific about our guilt. Moms raising children with special needs have an untapped resource of guilt for not only the atypical child but also his neurotypical siblings. I am talking about the other beautiful children we love with all our heart. These children are the ones who can get the short end of the stick.

I spent YEARS researching, learning, and advocating for my son with autism. Managing the therapies and behavioral charts, I constantly worried about him. Years. During those same years, I had three other children.

Three wonderful, awesome children, who didn't get their mother's full attention. I know I will be the cause of so much therapy when they are older. How do I justify this inattention, so that I don't feel like a horrible mother? In my mind, there is no justification or excuse for not giving every single child my undivided attention (which is physically impossible, right?).

Now, if my friend whose child has ADHD were to tell me she is a terrible mother because she has been focusing more on her special needs kid than her neurotypical kid, I would slap her in the mouth! I would tell her she is a great mother and is doing the best she can. I would tell her that her children feel her love and are learning so much about compassion, family, and dedication by just observing her. I would tell her studies have shown that kids with siblings who have special needs become more compassionate and empathetic human beings. I would remind her that just last week she took her neurotypical son on a date to the movies. I would tell her that her son does not feel less important than his sister (even if I don't know for sure). I would be kind to my friend. We are all doing the best we can, right?

We are our own worst enemy. Notice I would say all of that to someone else. But to me? I am telling myself I should have stayed up later and read with Joseph, instead of rubbing John's back so he would fall asleep easily. I should have sat on the floor next to Ann and played Barbies with her, instead of following James around to make sure he stayed on schedule. I should have shown more interest when John showed me his YouTube channel, instead of nodding and half listening while I figured out

Joseph's meds.

Shoulda. Coulda. Woulda.

Guilt for the siblings of a special needs child is massive. I agree with my kids when they say there are times that having a brother with ADHD sucks. It does suck sometimes. It also sucks when their brother with autism loses his shit, and we have to leave a party early. It sucks when a perfectly lovely family game of Monopoly turns into World War III because "someone" couldn't handle losing. It definitely sucks when their mom can't give them 100%, 75%, 50%, or even 25% of her time because she is attending to the small but mighty details of their special needs sibling.

The unfairness is constantly staring them right in their adorable faces. They are not blind to the unjustness of it all. It stinks when Ann cries, "It's unfair that he gets to sleep in Mommy's bed, and I don't." Or when John challenges, "He can quit baseball, but I can't quit track? Really?" And when Joseph asks, "Can't we leave him home? When he comes with us to the grocery store, everyone stares at us." I get it. That mom guilt will never go away.

We all think we are screwing everything up and ruining our children's lives. But, whaddaya gonna do? My vote is to have a glass of wine and remind myself that I am only human. And then have another glass of wine to make sure the point really sinks in!

Dear Loved Ones,

We feel like horrible parents for not giving each of our children 100% of our focus. Tell us what great kids we have. Tell us that our neurotypical children (don't call them that, though) are wonderful human beings. This is important: back up that statement with reasons why you feel that way. Reassure us that they are amazing because we are raising them to be that way! We need to hear we are the BEST mom for our children. We need to hear you say aloud that those little stinkers are blessed to have us as their mother!

It would also be awesome if you could watch our special needs child, so we can do something with our other kids that we wouldn't normally be able to do together, such as go to a loud concert! If our son with autism has a tantrum during his older brother's baseball game, take him to the snack bar with promises of ice cream, so we can completely focus on the huge hit #9 is going to get.

I know you want to watch your grandchild/niece/nephew in his first basketball game of the season, BUT SO DO WE! Sacrifice that first game and babysit our other children at home, so we can be his biggest cheerleader in the bleachers!
Thank you.

I PROMISE, WE ARE NOT TRYING TO BE DIFFICULT

I am not trying to be difficult when I ask if there are going to be blue balloons at your party, or if there will be music and, if so, how loud it will be. I am not being snotty when I ask if you will have a moon bounce at your kid's bar mitzvah. I ask because my son can't stand the noise of the moon bounce motor, will flip out at the sight of blue balloons, and will have a huge tantrum about music that is too loud. By asking these questions, I will know whether we will be attending your soiree, or whether we should regretfully decline your kind invitation and just send a gift.

Mom, I am not trying to be mean when you invite us for dinner, and I ask, "Are you going to make shepherd's pie again?" I am asking because the texture of the peas and potatoes sends John into a full-on gagging event. When I don't talk to any of the other moms at the playground, I am not trying to act bitchy. Trust me, I would love to chat, but I can't because James will try to jump, belly flop style, off the jungle gym, and I need to be ready to catch him. To clarify, sometimes I AM trying to act bitchy... but I guess you will never know which time is which! Hmmmmmm.

I am not trying to be rude when I interrupt your story every five seconds to check my phone. It's just that we have a new sitter, and she didn't seem very confident when I left her tonight. The nighttime routine can be hard for someone new.

Uncle Pete, when I roll my eyes at you when you state for the sixth time in an afternoon, "This kid just needs to get the belt", well, in that instance, I am rolling my eyes because that is a super annoying thing to say and will never happen. Sorry, not sorry.

Dear Loved Ones,

Don't give up on us if we seem wound too tight or if we are acting weird or "funny". We are just living our life the best way we know how. Trust us, we are not trying to be difficult. In fact, we are actually trying to make life easier for you, and ourselves, by being proactive and staying ahead of the game. So, you are welcome.

Please work on this response: "No worries!" Say it again. "No worries!"

This should be your reply to pretty much everything we say to you.

- "We won't be able to make dinner."
"No worries."

- "James is having a rough day, so we will need to cancel our lunch plans."
"No worries."

- "I have to leave your party before 'Happy Birthday' is sung because it gets too loud for my sensory-sensitive kids."
"No worries."

It is so easy to say and puts us at ease. By saying this, you are actually saying you understand us and love us. Thank you.

FRIENDS? WHAT ARE THEY?

Here is something that has taken me forty years to learn: if you want a good friend, you need to be a good friend. In my younger years, being a good friend wasn't an issue because my only distractions were school and how to get a zit tamed before the big dance. My bestie and I would sit on my bed and talk for hours about which New Kids on the Block singer was our soulmate (Joey, duh). We knew everything about one another. We got our first period at the same time, for heaven's sake!

Girls, more than ever, need friends. Our self-esteem depends on it! I USED to be a good friend. I used to be there for my friends. I would jump to a friend's rescue by giving her my fitted red shirt, so her boobs looked bigger for her date that night. I'd go on a double date to the movies with a boy's ugly friend, so she could go out with her crush. I miss those easy, straightforward friendships.

Before my kids started kicking my ass with every

diagnosis under the sun, this was me:

"Yes, let's grab drinks!"

"Yes, let's go away for the weekend!"

"Yes, I am SO funny!"

"Yes, let's run five miles and talk about our hopes and dreams!"

"Yes, let's be besties and never leave each other!"

After my kids started kicking my ass with every diagnosis under the sun, this is me:

"Sorry, I can't grab drinks because I can't find a sitter who can handle these fools."

"Sorry, I can't go on a girls' trip because I would rather sleep for an entire weekend by myself than stay up all night partying."

"No, I don't care about running anymore or about anything, really, so just go on without me."

Truth is, I'm not a "bestie" kind of girl anymore. In fact, I would drop your ass in a second if any one of my kids even hinted at wanting to watch a movie with me.

Inevitably, friends took a back seat while I struggled to stay afloat with my newly diagnosed special needs family. I stopped answering the phone and they stopped calling. When I got to a point where I could take a breath, I realized I hadn't talked to my friends in months. I couldn't, for the life of me, figure out where they went. The thoughts in my head about this situation went like this:

"Well, f*ck them! They have no idea what my life is like! They have no clue what I go through every day with these kids! Trying to get Joseph to actually get into the school building? Trying to calm John down when he flips out because his Xbox time limit has been reached? Getting James to put on a pair of socks without having a colossal meltdown? Have them try, for one day, to live my life. I'm sorry I didn't call you back, I have been busy raising my CHILDREN DIAGNOSED WITH AUTISM, ADHD, SENSORY PROCESSING DISORDER, ANXIETY, DEPRESSION, AND OPPOSITIONAL DEFIANT DISORDER!!! They should be ashamed of themselves. No one asks how I am doing? Or what they can do to help me? Screw them! They aren't good friends. I don't need them."

After *years* of therapy, I see things differently now. I realized that I distanced myself, too. I put myself in a safe cocoon where no one could touch me. I believed I was the only one with a tough life. I believed their lives were hunky-dory, while I was drowning in mine. Instead of talking to them about it, I withdrew. Truth is, we all go through tough times and they were probably going through their own shit, that I didn't ask about. Those friends are still in my life and I respect the role they play in it. They are A LOT of fun and make me laugh so hard I usually end up peeing my pants.

My husband and I began making more friends as our children got older. These relationships are based around our beautiful families. I feel blessed to have them in my life. My friend, Mia, will help talk James out of the car and onto the baseball field, with promises of cookies and brownies. Aiden will order the game truck an hour early on his son's birthday, so James and his best bud can play video games on the massive trailer parked outside the house before the crowd comes and it becomes too noisy for him. They will pick up a kid from school, babysit last minute, and truly understand and accept my family for who we are. Truly blessed.

This chapter was supposed to be about how moms raising kids with invisible special needs don't have a lot of friends because we are too busy taking care of our families. But the truth is, we are all busy raising our kids, special needs or not. We can all regretfully decline a dinner invitation because "life is too hard". But maybe we shouldn't.

Next time, maybe I'll say "yes" when asked to meet for a drink. Maybe I'll move out of my comfort zone and try to get a semblance of a social life back. It's time to stop making excuses and start living a little more.

Dear Loved Ones,

Please remind us that, every once in a while, we can go back to that pre-kid, pre-worry life and just enjoy "being". Tell us that we should go out with friends. Implore us to enjoy and celebrate the fact that we have gotten this far, and we are still trucking!

While we are learning to get back out into the "friend world", be gentle with us. We aren't going to change overnight, but we will try to see the big picture and that we do, in fact, need our friends. Don't give up on us. We are trying our best to learn to balance it all.

If you are worried about our mental health, discuss your concerns with us privately. No need to stage an intervention or make a scene. Text us, on the down low, the name of a doctor or therapist that you heard was really good. Then, let us take it from there. If we are ready, we will make an appointment and if not, we will put that name and number in a safe place for when we are. There is a possibility we will find this annoying and want you to mind your own business, but know that, deep down, we feel your love.

Thank you.

DO YOURSELF A FAVOR, POP A PILL

Don't freak out. I am not saying EVERYONE should be taking an antidepressant: just mothers of children with invisible special needs... and every man and woman over the age of forty. We should all be on Zoloft, Paxil, Prozac, or whatever the "Happy Pill" du jour is. I'm only half joking. To be clear, I am not a doctor and should not be listened to about medical advice at all (or any advice, some would say). But, in my humble opinion, if you weren't depressed before you were forty, you are bound to become disheartened as you get older. Trust me. The wrinkles, gray hair, body aches, floppy boobs, and sagging butt will make you depressed. You have no choice but to feel like crap when you notice your cellulite has tripled overnight. The relentless pressure for women to be too perfect is suffocating. The bar is set so high and impossible to meet, yet we just keep trying. I'm exhausted!

Now, add raising children with special needs into

the mix. I read an interesting statistic from The Family Caregiver Alliance that "20% of family caregivers suffer from depression, twice the rate of the general population." This issue is real and scary. Taking care of a child with special needs takes every ounce of energy and patience we have. It takes every piece of our heart, soul, and spirit EVERY. SINGLE. DAY. Waking up in the morning and already knowing what lies ahead of us—physical abuse, verbal attacks, school issues, emotional upset, to name just a few possibilities—is so demoralizing. Yet we do it. We get up each day and do it over and over again. We do it because we love these little bastards! It takes a toll on us that is not always seen by the outsider.

I know so many moms who must deal with their ADHD kid bouncing off the walls when their medicine wears off. The lull between one medication ending and the other kicking in can feel like years to a mom. My friend called me crying one day and told me she couldn't handle it anymore. It was too hard for her to deal with all of this. The kids, the husband, the therapies, the sticker charts, all of it. She told me she cried all the time and that she was miserable. I told her Zoloft and psychotherapy saved me (because I will tell anyone who will listen my medication list, diagnoses, and any other personal detail about my life—it's a boundary problem I need to work on). Don't get me wrong: I still cry and can be mean to my husband—but definitely not as much as before!

I have another friend who complains constantly about being depressed, but she won't talk to her doctor about it. That is so dumb. SO DUMB. The women who are on meds for depression or anxiety, or both, should shout it from the rooftops because it is NOT a bad thing. The stupid stigma of being "crazy" is still there, but f*ck the stigma. Want to REALLY blow minds? Go to a therapist! I go once a week, and it's a chance for me to say things I could never say aloud to anyone else. It's also a chance to talk about my favorite subject: ME! I could talk for hours about me. Just ask my friends.

Those of us on meds and in therapy feel better and want others to feel better, too. The combination of therapy and medication is what helped me sort my shit out and be the best person I could be, not just for me, but for my family. Lecture over.

Dear Loved Ones,

Tell us we should talk to our doctors. Gently nudge us to talk to someone... anyone. Tell us that Harvard Health reports "23% of women in their 40s and 50s take antidepressants, a higher percentage than any other group." Enlighten us by telling us that, "Moms of children with mental illness are two to three times more likely to be depressed than mothers of healthy children." (Barkley 1992).

Tell us that it is Ok, even cool, to get help. So that we don't have an excuse to back out, babysit the kids for us while we go to the doctor's appointment or offer to drive us there.

We may roll our eyes or tell you to shove off. Don't give up! It's better for everyone if we are taking the medication our doctor prescribed to us. Reassure us that these meds do not make us "failures". They aren't going to turn us into zombies or stop us from feeling anything at all. It will just help us be more ourselves.

Thank you.

P.S. Have you thought about going on meds yourself? Just sayin'.

THE MAGIC ANSWER

I am always reading self-help books. In fact, right now I have four on my nightstand, two in my office, and one on my bookshelf. I love the idea of learning ways to be a better mother, wife, and human. I never want to stop learning (Nerd Alert)!

When James was diagnosed with autism, I spent hours reading books about every technique, theory, and practice that might alleviate some of his symptoms. I was desperate to know what he needed and how I could help him. These books gave me insight into a world I knew nothing about and taught me so much. I also learned there is no single correct answer. It doesn't exist. What works for one kid will not work for another. The magic answer for this unique, beautiful, wonderful, smart, loud, impulsive, worried, scared, mighty kid of mine? Me, his mom. I'm his answer. Dads, therapists, teachers, siblings, grandparents, aunts and uncles are all grand, but it is Mom who will make it all better. It's Mom who knows that James needs to swing in his swing for seven minutes before he starts to calm down. It's Mom who knows that the weighted blanket works for John but not Joseph. Mom knows the songs, and in what order, they are to be sung at bedtime.

Let me clear: The idea that I'm his magic answer terrifies me. I'm not a "magic" anything. Hell, I'm a forty-year-old woman who still laughs when someone trips. I still giggle when someone says, "duty", for God's sake! The fact that this beautiful, little human is depending so much, on me, is incredible! I am in awe of who God has entrusted me with and will do my best not to let Him down!

I believe all moms feel the pressure of being their kids' magic answer. Moms of special needs kids? Just add an extra ton, or so, of weight.

The books I read are actually good for something else, too: the fact that there are books about school refusal and sensory issues is proof that there are other kids who have these challenges, which reminds me I am not alone. Because feeling alone sucks. Reading about other parents' successes and failures, gives me hope and comfort. So, I will continue to absorb all the anecdotes and bits of wisdom I can, before my vision goes (is it me, or did the font get smaller?) and my brain cells burn out.

Dear Loved Ones,

Please don't hand us articles to read about the negative effects of too much screen time for children. We are aware. The email you forwarded about the high number of children with unmanaged ADHD who go to prison is not helpful, because we already knew it. I know you mean well, but telling us the nasty side effects of Ritalin (which you know our son is on) shows us you don't believe we have done our research.

Giving us these "helpful articles" is actually insulting. It makes us feel like you believe we haven't done our homework for our own child. Do you really believe we would give our child something without researching the shit out of it first? We know everything there is to know about our child's disability. And, what we don't know, we will learn from our doctor.

From now on, send us an email about how wine makes moms happier, with an invite attached to grab a drink this weekend. An article about mothers of special needs kids aging slower than moms of neurotypical kids is another one I want to read. Keep those articles coming and throw the other articles in the trash.

Thank you.

THE STRUGGLE IS REAL

I don't want this chapter to scare anyone. Well, it won't scare moms whose kids have an invisible special need, because we live it every day. It may, however, scare the laypersons out there. You are going to want to call 911 after you read this, but please don't.

If you have someone you love with a neurological disorder like ADHD or oppositional defiant disorder, you know that anger is a pretty well-known emotion in the household. John has such a low frustration tolerance and is triggered easily. James has a hard time practicing self-control, which makes anger his go-to response. Joseph blows up when I least expect it. I feel bad for them sometimes because I can see the anger escalating before my very eyes. I try to speak calmly and prepare myself for what is about to unfold, but I never really know what's coming.

Whichever son is raging, will come at me with full-on violence. He will charge me with fists clenched, ready to rumble. Right now, I am at least fifty pounds heavier than each of them, giving me the upper hand. In a few years, that won't be the case. We have holes in our doors from Joseph's fists and craters in the walls from James' feet. John has thrown things at my head at top speed. I have been punched, kicked, and had my hair pulled. My boys don't always realize what they are doing as it is happening. Actually, they may know but don't care at that exact moment. All of this from the children I love with all my heart.

Some may say I am in danger and should not allow this behavior in my home. My reply to them would be, "He isn't your son, and you don't get it. I will do whatever it takes to help my son work through his issues. Now, back off!"

Shortly after an explosion, the perpetrator will calm down and begin to breathe normally again. There is no apology or remorse, just exhaustion from the ordeal. I realize as I type this that I sound like an abused woman. In a way, I guess I am. My plan is to handle it for as long as I can. I will continue to pray that, with therapy and medication, my sons will learn to manage their emotions. Is it right? Maybe not. Are they my sons? Yes. There you go.

It is hard to imagine anyone else having these scenes play out in their home. When the chaos ends and I'm by myself, I feel alone on an island where no one understands my life. I think parents with kids who have these disorders do, in fact, have these scenes as well, but no one talks about it. Why would I tell people that my beautiful son can act like a wild animal at times and try to hurt me? I don't want anyone to know that side of him. I don't want anyone to see that my precious child could do those things to his own mother. My son is more than this dysregulation of emotions. I want people to see his sweet, kind heart. I want them to see the wonderful person he is.

I chose to write this chapter because of something that just happened to me this morning. Earlier today, I walked into the kitchen and saw my son holding a kitchen knife, demanding he get his phone back, even though he had used up his daily screen time allotment. I calmly told him that knives aren't funny and to put it back. I acted like I was not at all interested in his words or actions. I sounded as if I were just bored of him. But inside, secretly, I wondered if he could or would actually stab me. I am embarrassed that I had that thought about my son, but I don't believe I am the only parent of a child with ADHD, oppositional defiant disorder, or autism who has thought something like that. I can't be the only one.

I am not condoning my child's actions or saying this is how anyone should act, but this is the world I live in. I am Ok with talking about my world if it means my kid has a chance of being understood. Someone once told me that I will instinctively know when/if I am in real danger. I just pray that it never comes to that. But I am not naïve enough to think it can't.

Dear Loved Ones,

Please understand that this is happening in homes all around you. To those who are horrified and appalled that I would accept that type of behavior from my child, I say, "Back off! You wouldn't survive a day in my shoes."

Just know that we are dealing with scenes in our homes that you could not imagine. Throughout all of this, we are still volunteering at the community bake sale, being the 2nd grade classroom mom, and working outside the home.

We may never tell you the ugly shit that goes on when our front door closes. Just know it is happening and we are struggling. Tell us to call you when things get nasty at home and that you will watch the kids while we take a walk. Help us to feel less ashamed of our children who act out in anger. Make us feel like we are not alone... and that our children won't grow up to be ax murderers.

Here's what NOT to do: do not try to "make us feel better" by telling us about your son, Eugene, who can get into trouble, too. Don't compare Eugene refusing to wear his ascot for the golf tournament to my knife-wielding son. Not a good comparison. If you do, I feel it would be understood, by a jury, if I strangled you with Eugene's ascot.

Thank you.

FROM ACTIVE DUTY TO RESERVES

To Whom it may Concern,

I, Julie Falcone, of somewhat sound mind and ok-ish body, hereby decree that I NEED A BREAK. After the many years of being everything to everyone, I will be resigning from my fulltime position as "Mom, Mommy, Mother, Mama, MOOOOOOM" effective immediately. Please accept this letter as notice of my resignation from this extremely demanding job. The last fifteen years have been filled with many memories, some I will recall fondly, and others I hope to forget. As you know, my sole job has been to keep the "Falcone Family Train" chugging like a well-oiled machine. After the many years of:

- Breastfeeding (which my boobs will never forgive me for),
- potty training,
- cleaning runny noses (with boogers, the likes of

which you have never seen before),

- wiping butts (and then cleaning their nasty underwear when they thought they could wipe their own butts),
- advocating for IEPs and 504s (using words like "functional spontaneous communication"),
- handling phone calls from teachers,
- driving kids to doctors' offices in different cities, suburbs, and states,
- navigating bedtimes like an FBI hostage negotiator,
- becoming an expert in insurance, pharmacology, and psychology,
- all the while functioning on very little sleep,

I would like to thank you for the opportunity to raise these humans. Fortunately, a new opportunity, with better hours and more flexibility, has become available to me. Good luck and God Speed.

Your extremely worn-out employee,

Julie Falcone

Oh, you want to know what my new job is? Well, it is very similar to my old job EXCEPT the hours are better! I scored the position of "Parent Consultant", also referred to as, "Special Needs Mom Whose Children are Doing Well-Enough". Cue balloons falling from the ceiling, confetti everywhere, and applause galore!

I don't know when or how it happened, but each fruit of my loins is doing well! They are managing their issues and needing me less as a boss and more as a consultant. What I am saying is…my job has become part-time. Well, not my whole job, but the part where I go from crisis to crisis, putting out fire after fire. There are fewer messes to clean up, figuratively and literally. My babies are growing up and becoming more independent! Don't get me wrong: they may always have their issues, but they have begun to use the skills they have been taught to work through them. I am still there to guide them, but they are taking the reins more and more each day. I feel free! I feel light! I feel excited!

After one month into my new job: I feel useless! I feel sad! I feel lost!

It is a bit cliché to say, "Now that the kids are grown, who am I?" But, in reality, that's *exactly* what I am asking myself. Who the hell am I, if I am not the stay-at-home mother of children with invisible special needs? Please don't tell me that my job as a mother is never over or that there is no more important job in the world. Duh and duh. That is not what I am saying. I am questioning, "Now that I am no longer on therapy and doctor appointment duty, what am I supposed to do with all this extra brain space and energy?" I mean, I was NEEDED for my kids to function. Literally, function.

Now, I feel I have no purpose. There is no meaning to my actions any longer. Am I just a lazy woman who doesn't work? Am I just the woman who cleans the house, walks the dog, and occasionally makes dinner for her family? That sounds sad and embarrassing. I MUST be more than that. I HAVE to be more than that. PLEASE let me be more than that.

I started taking up new hobbies to find my next aspiration. I bought myself a compound miter saw and installed wainscoting up the stairs and hallway. I put up crown molding in the bedroom all by myself. I refinished and repainted old furniture. I am all up in this house! I enrolled in martial arts classes, took cooking lessons and volunteered for a slew of organizations. My husband and I even attempted dance lessons. Sadly, none of these endeavors spoke to my heart in the way I had hoped.

When I brought up this dilemma to my therapist, she asked me what I did for fun before I was a mother. Umm, let me think back to, what feels like, a lifetime ago. Fun? Fun was drinking in a bar with thirty of my closest friends, getting black out drunk and kissing boys. I imagine a middle age woman slurring her words does not come off as cute as the twenty-somethings. Instead of a cute boy, I would score an ambulance ride to the Stroke Department of the local hospital. So, cross "adorable drunk" off the list of possible options.

A chance to reinvent yourself sounds cool in theory, but the pressure of picking who I want to be is almost too much to handle. After months of lessons, home projects, and classes, I learned that trying to identify the "new me" is exhausting! I realized, after being cut from the bowling league on account of too many gutter balls, that I don't have to decide today. There's no need to rush this next chapter in my life. I should, in fact, enjoy the journey.

Dear Loved Ones,

When our kids get older and more independent, we will have an identity crisis. Let us have it.

Don't tease us about our latest "fad" or say things like, "Jesus, get a job. You have too much time on your hands."

Don't analyze us and try to find out what feelings we are avoiding as we rearrange the entire house (or whatever our project du jour is). Just understand that we don't know who we are right now and it's not your job to figure it out.

Give us time to let go of the mother we were and figure out the mother we are going to be. Just tell us how great the house looks or how martial arts is a beautiful discipline. Give us the time and space we need to work things out.

Every second of our lives since we became mothers has been given to our children. We have a lot of feelings, emotions, and thoughts to work through. Feel free to recommend a good therapist.

Thank you.

IF YOU COULD SEE THEM NOW

My cousin, Katie, is one of my biggest fans. This year our families rented a house in North Carolina for two weeks. There were seven adults and eight children staying under the same roof. We were having a great time just being together. At the end of our first week, Katie came to me with a worried look on her face. She put her hands on my shoulders, looked straight into my eyes and said, "I think you have Munchausen syndrome by proxy!" Huh? When I looked at her blankly, she explained that Munchausen syndrome is a mental illness where a mother makes up fake symptoms or causes real symptoms to make it look like her child is sick. She wasn't serious, of course, but she pointed out that my children were behaving so well: participating in every activity, happily conversing with the adults, and helping the younger kids with anything they needed. Basically, my children were angels the entire vacation! She lovingly said that she can't imagine that these are the same children I would cry for hours to her about. Her words made happy tears run down my cheeks, because without realizing it, my children were thriving. Not merely surviving, THRIVING!

If you would have told me while we were in the thick of all that comes with ADHD, autism, sensory processing disorder, depression, anxiety and oppositional defiant disorder that one day I would be able to take my family on vacation and have zero fires to put out, I would have sadly shaken my head and thought "Never gonna happen". I truly believed that no matter how much love and work I put into my kids, it would never be enough. I felt defeated. I had accepted that my life would always be in crisis mode. I am so grateful to have been wrong.

There was a shift. Not all at once, but so slowly that I didn't even see it happening. James' outbursts were happening less often. John's medication was hitting the mark and he hadn't become aggressive in days. Joseph's teachers were telling us how kind and funny he was. I was able to spend quality time with Ann without being interrupted by the demands of others. For the first time I felt a sense of calm and peace. I felt...hopeful!

Each family has different challenges and most won't be wrapped up in a cute little bow at the end. My children will continue to work on using the skills they have learned to handle situations that may trigger them. Heck, we all should! I believe they will be Ok. My husband and I will focus on having a relationship that is not tethered to the children, but one based on mutual love and respect of each other as individuals, instead of just parents. We will be Ok.

Let me be clear: my life is not rainbows and unicorns all of a sudden, nor will it ever be. But, unlike in the past, I have hope.

When I think about the moms right now who are in the throes of diagnoses, evaluations, therapies, traumas and crises, my heart hurts. It hurts not just because of what they are outwardly dealing with, but because I remember the feelings of helplessness and hopelessness that can be all consuming. I have learned many things from raising my children for the past 15 years. The mantra I keep close to my heart is, "It won't always be like this." To me, that statement is about having hope. It will be Ok.

Dear Loved Ones,

Encourage us to have hope. Assure us that it will not always be like this. Remind us of a time when we thought we had hit rock bottom, only to come out stronger in the end. Tell us the story about how a few years ago, our child wouldn't look you in the eye and now he does it without having to be reminded. Point out that our child was communicating with only grunts and tantrums a year ago and, because of our persistence and his hard work, he now talks in sentences. It is easy to forget how far our family has come when we are in the midst of a new crisis. Encourage us to dig deep and see the light at the end of the tunnel. Because there is a light there.

The hope is not that our child be "fixed". No, he is perfectly made. Our hope is that the world can see and understand his perfection. Then again, screw the world. If they can't see it, that's their loss. He's got me, his dad, and you, my wonderful family and friends.

Thank you.

**Thank you for reading.
A short review would be greatly appreciated.**

ACKNOWLEDGEMENTS

I would like to thank my husband, Nick Falcone, for enthusiastically pushing me to stay on track, otherwise my ADHD would have won out and there would be an unfinished manuscript collecting dust on our bookshelf. Thank you to my children, Gabe, Matt, Lucy and Chris for permitting me to recount stories that did not always paint them in the best light. You bring me so much joy. Even though this book has two hundred pages filled with stories of our struggles, please know I could write *millions* of pages about our triumphs! Thanks to my talented daughter who illustrated the cover of this book, with whom I am proud as punch. To my sister, Carin Rassier, for continuously reminding me why I was writing this book every time I threatened to quit. Shout out to my beta readers for giving me honest and productive feedback. Thank you to Maggie McCabe, for my website and author photos and using photoshop liberally. Will, Luke, Hope, Michael, Mia, Jordan and Nathan, thanks for being the best nieces and nephews ever. (Look, your name is in a book!). Lastly, thank you Grammy and Poppy and Mom-Mom and Pop-Pop, for always being there for us. We are blessed beyond belief.

GLOSSARY

ADD: This refers to "Attention Deficit Disorder," an older term for ADHD. This term has been replaced with the term "ADHD" to include all presentations of this disorder.

ADHD-Combined Type: A subtype of ADHD characterized by both inattentive and hyperactive/impulsive symptoms of ADHD.

ADHD-Predominantly Hyperactive-Impulsive: A subtype of ADHD characterized by impulsivity and hyperactivity but lacking the symptoms of inattention.

ADHD-Predominantly Inattentive: A subtype of ADHD characterized by inattentive symptoms, but lacking hyperactivity and impulsivity symptoms.

ADHD: This refers to Attention-Deficit/Hyperactivity Disorder, the official name given this condition by the American Psychiatric Association. It is described in the Diagnostic and Statistical Manual of Mental Disorders as a persistent condition that impairs functioning or development, and characterized by chronic inattention, hyperactivity, and often impulsivity.

Antidepressant. A drug used to treat depression.

Anxiety disorder. A chronic condition that causes anxiety so severe it interferes with your life. Some people with depression also have overlapping anxiety disorder.

Applied behavior analysis (ABA): A therapeutic approach that encourages desired behavior and skills. This includes positive behavior support (PBS) that aims to identify the reason for problematic behaviors and replace them with more appropriate behaviors.

Autism: A developmental disorder of variable severity that is characterized by difficulty in social interaction and communication and by restricted or repetitive patterns of thought and behavior.

Clinical Depression: A mental health disorder characterized by persistently depressed mood or loss of interest in activities, causing significant impairment in daily life.

Co-Existing Conditions: When two or more mental health conditions are present in the same individual, they are said to be co-existing (also called co-occurring or co-morbid). For example, ADHD can co-exist with depression or anxiety.

Depression (major depressive disorder) is a common and serious medical illness that negatively affects how you feel, the way you think and how you act.

Early Intervention Services (EI): Free, federally funded state services for children younger than 3 who have, or are likely to have, a developmental delay. Each child has an Individual Family Service Plan (IFSP) describing the child's needs and services, which may include some of the behavioral and physical therapies described in this list.

Executive Function: Mental skills that allow us to control and coordinate other mental functions and abilities, such as planning or task completion. This deficit is common in those with ADHD.

Fine motor delay is when a child is not able to use their hands and fingers to hold, manipulate, and use objects when the child is at the right age to do these things.

Impulsivity: Acting with little or no thought of the consequences or reacting rapidly without considering the negative consequences of the reaction.

Inattention: Failure to pay attention to a specified object or task.

Individualized Education Plan (IEP): A written document that describes the educational goals at school, and the methods of achieving these goals, for eligible children with disabilities under IDEA. This plan is based on the child's current level of performance.

Intervention: A structured process (or action) that has the effect of modifying an individual's behavior, cognition, or emotional state.

Negative Self-Talk: Negative inner dialogue that brings out emotions such as guilt, fear, pessimism, anger, frustration, anxiety and depression. These thoughts often damage self-esteem and can appear in times of increased stress or emotional turmoil.

Neurologist: A health care professional trained to diagnose and manage brain disorders.

Non-stimulant Medication: A medication that has been approved to treat ADHD—generally considered second-line medication—prescribed to those who have an incomplete response or no response to stimulants, cannot tolerate stimulants, or have certain co-existing psychiatric conditions.

Occupational Therapist: A licensed health care professional who provides therapy centered on sensory integration to address the physical, behavioral, and emotional effects of ADHD, and identifies goals to help the child succeed at school and at home.

Oppositional defiant disorder (ODD): is a condition where children have disruptive and oppositional behavior that is particularly directed towards authority figures, such as parents or teachers.

Perception: The meaning the brain gives to sensory input. Sensations are objective; perception is subjective.

Physical therapy (PT): Strategies to help with movement and motion, such as toe-walking, repetitive movements, weak muscles, and difficulty planning and carrying out actions. PT also improves motor skills such as balance, coordination, and walking.

Proprioception: From the Latin for "one's own." Refers to perception of sensation from the muscles and joints. Proprioceptive input tells the brain when and how muscles are contracting and stretching, and when and how the joints are bending, extending or being pulled or compressed. This information enables the brain to know where each part of the body is and how it is moving. Sensory input: The streams of neural impulses flowing from the sense receptors in the body to the spinal cord and brain.

Psychiatrist. A medical doctor (MD or DO) who specializes in treating mental health disorders. Because psychiatrists are doctors, they can prescribe drugs like antidepressants.

Psychologist. A non-MD professional (PhD or PsyD) who specializes in the treatment of mental or emotional disorders.

Sensory integration: The many parts of the nervous system work together so that a person can interact with the environment effectively and experience appropriate satisfaction.

Sensory Processing Disorder: is a condition in which the brain and nervous system are unable to correctly receive, organize and process information coming in from the senses, causing learning and behavioral problems.

Speech therapy: Focuses on communication skills to help

children express themselves better, which can decrease frustration and improve behavior. Speech therapy can help children participate in conversations, follow directions, write, and ask for help. Children who don't speak may learn to use gestures, pictures, and sign language to communicate.

Stimulant Medication: Medication that "stimulate" (increase) certain activity in the body's central nervous system, including the production and activity of neurotransmitters. Most medications approved for the treatment of ADHD are stimulant medications. When taken as prescribed, they generally help improve the symptoms of ADHD by promoting alertness, awareness, and the ability to focus.

Token Economy System: A behavior modification system in which a student earns tokens for exhibiting the desired behavior. The tokens are exchanged at a later time for a reinforcer which is typically selected by the student.

.

RESOURCE PAGE

*Resources I have personally used

* The Autism Community in Action (TACA): TACA provides education, support and hope to families living with autism. www.taca.org

* Children and Adults with Attention Deficit/ Hyperactivity Disorder (CHADD): CHADD provides information, support, and advocacy to families and individuals with ADHD. www.chadd.org

* **"Taking Charge of ADHD: The Complete, Authoritative Guide for Parents"** by Russell Barkley. (Third edition. Amazon paperback $12.22)

* **"The Explosive Child: A New Approach For Understanding And Parenting Easily Frustrated, Chronically Inflexible Children"** by Ross Greene. (Amazon, paperback $12.89)

* **"What to Expect When Parenting Children with ADHD: A 9-step plan to master the struggles and triumphs of parenting a child with ADHD"** by Penny Williams. (Amazon, paperback $15.95. $8.99 Kindle edition)

* Happy Mama Conference and Retreat: A retreat for moms of kids with invisible special needs. https://if-mama-aint-happy.com

* Camp Pegasus: Intensive social-coping skills therapy/training program disguised in a super-fun day camp structure. Haverford, PA. www.camppegasus.com

American Academy of Child and Adolescent Psychiatry (AACAP): promotes the healthy development of children, adolescents, and families through advocacy, education, and research. www.aacap.org

The National Institute of Mental Health: transforms the understanding and treatment of mental illnesses through basic and clinical research, paving the way for prevention, recovery, and cure. www.nih.gov

The Child Mind Institute: Empowers parents, professionals, and policy makers to support children when and where they need it most. www.childmind.org

*****Empowering Parents**: Parenting help for child behavior problems. Home of The Total Transformation® Program. Tools to manage disrespect, defiance, motivation, and more. www.empoweringparents.com

Star Institute: To improve the quality of life of children, adolescents and adults with SPD, and their families. www.starinstitute.com

Anxiety and Depression Association of America: ADAA's mission focuses on improving quality of life for those with anxiety, depression, OCD, PTSD, and co-occurring disorders through education, practice, and research. www.adaa.org

"The Essential Guide to Raising Complex Kids with ADHD, Anxiety, and More" by Elaine Taylor-Klaus. (Amazon, paperback $17.87. Kindle edition $15.89)

Center for Young Women's Health and Young Men's Health: These websites provide information targeted at parents of adolescents, including guides on how to support children suffering from depression and eating disorders. http://youngwomenshealth.org/parents/ and http://youngmenshealthsite.org/parents/

WORKS CITED

Barkley, R. (2013). *Taking Charge of ADHD, Third Edition.* 3rd ed. Guilford Publications, Incorporated.

Curry, A., Metzger, K., Pfeiffer, M., Elliott, M., Winston, F. and Power, T. (2017). Motor Vehicle Crash Risk Among Adolescents and Young Adults With Attention-Deficit/Hyperactivity Disorder. *JAMA Pediatrics*, 171(8), p.756.

Wilens, T. (2011). A Sobering Fact: ADHD Leads to Substance Abuse. *Journal of the American Academy of Child & Adolescent Psychiatry*, 50(1), pp.6-8.

ABOUT THE AUTHOR

 Julie Falcone is a mother raising four children diagnosed with a myriad of neurological disorders. She has spent the last fifteen years becoming an unofficial teacher, doctor, pharmacist, police officer, bouncer, therapist, scientist, psychiatrist, and insurance agent to advocate for her special needs children.

She feels invincible any day she gets to pee in private or eat a meal sitting down. When she's not being swallowed up whole by her very amazing, but needy children, husband, and dogs, she...well, she can't say, because it has never happened before.

Her goal is to help mothers raising children with invisible special needs feel seen and valued.

Made in the USA
Middletown, DE
15 December 2020

28499611R00118